NT-60  NATIONAL TEACHER EXAMINATION SERIES

*This is your*
*PASSBOOK for...*

# School Food Service Supervisor

*Test Preparation Study Guide*
*Questions & Answers*

# COPYRIGHT NOTICE

This book is SOLELY intended for, is sold ONLY to, and its use is RESTRICTED to individual, bona fide applicants or candidates who qualify by virtue of having seriously filed applications for appropriate license, certificate, professional and/or promotional advancement, higher school matriculation, scholarship, or other legitimate requirements of education and/or governmental authorities.

This book is NOT intended for use, class instruction, tutoring, training, duplication, copying, reprinting, excerption, or adaptation, etc., by:

1) Other publishers
2) Proprietors and/or Instructors of "Coaching" and/or Preparatory Courses
3) Personnel and/or Training Divisions of commercial, industrial, and governmental organizations
4) Schools, colleges, or universities and/or their departments and staffs, including teachers and other personnel
5) Testing Agencies or Bureaus
6) Study groups which seek by the purchase of a single volume to copy and/or duplicate and/or adapt this material for use by the group as a whole without having purchased individual volumes for each of the members of the group
7) Et al.

Such persons would be in violation of appropriate Federal and State statutes.

PROVISION OF LICENSING AGREEMENTS – Recognized educational, commercial, industrial, and governmental institutions and organizations, and others legitimately engaged in educational pursuits, including training, testing, and measurement activities, may address request for a licensing agreement to the copyright owners, who will determine whether, and under what conditions, including fees and charges, the materials in this book may be used them. In other words, a licensing facility exists for the legitimate use of the material in this book on other than an individual basis. However, it is asseverated and affirmed here that the material in this book CANNOT be used without the receipt of the express permission of such a licensing agreement from the Publishers. Inquiries re licensing should be addressed to the company, attention rights and permissions department.

All rights reserved, including the right of reproduction in whole or in part, in any form or by any means, electronic or mechanical, including photocopying, recording, or by any information storage and retrieval system, without permission in writing from the Publisher.

Copyright © 2025 by
## National Learning Corporation

212 Michael Drive, Syosset, NY 11791
(516) 921-8888 • www.passbooks.com
E-mail: info@passbooks.com

# PASSBOOK® SERIES

THE *PASSBOOK® SERIES* has been created to prepare applicants and candidates for the ultimate academic battlefield – the examination room.

At some time in our lives, each and every one of us may be required to take an examination – for validation, matriculation, admission, qualification, registration, certification, or licensure.

Based on the assumption that every applicant or candidate has met the basic formal educational standards, has taken the required number of courses, and read the necessary texts, the *PASSBOOK® SERIES* furnishes the one special preparation which may assure passing with confidence, instead of failing with insecurity. Examination questions – together with answers – are furnished as the basic vehicle for study so that the mysteries of the examination and its compounding difficulties may be eliminated or diminished by a sure method.

This book is meant to help you pass your examination provided that you qualify and are serious in your objective.

The entire field is reviewed through the huge store of content information which is succinctly presented through a provocative and challenging approach – the question-and-answer method.

A climate of success is established by furnishing the correct answers at the end of each test.

You soon learn to recognize types of questions, forms of questions, and patterns of questioning. You may even begin to anticipate expected outcomes.

You perceive that many questions are repeated or adapted so that you can gain acute insights, which may enable you to score many sure points.

You learn how to confront new questions, or types of questions, and to attack them confidently and work out the correct answers.

You note objectives and emphases, and recognize pitfalls and dangers, so that you may make positive educational adjustments.

Moreover, you are kept fully informed in relation to new concepts, methods, practices, and directions in the field.

You discover that you are actually taking the examination all the time: you are preparing for the examination by "taking" an examination, not by reading extraneous and/or supererogatory textbooks.

In short, this PASSBOOK®, used directedly, should be an important factor in helping you to pass your test.

# NATIONAL TEACHER / PRAXIS EXAMINATIONS (NTE)

## INTRODUCTION

I. WHAT ARE THE PRAXIS EXAMINATIONS?

The Praxis Series Examinations comprise standardized tests that measure the academic achievement and proficiency of teaching applicants. Developed and administered by the Educational Testing Service (ETS), these exams evaluate the ability and knowledge of college seniors completing teacher education programs and advanced candidates who have received additional professional training in specific fields.

State departments of education and local school systems in this country that do not administer their own examinations for teaching positions may require teaching applicants to submit scores on the National Teacher Praxis Examination Series. These professional assessments of beginning teachers are designed to provide objective measurements of the knowledge, skills and abilities required in the teaching profession. These test results are then used for certifying teachers as initial, qualifying, validating, statutory, incremental, promotional and/or supervisory.

Additionally, many colleges use the Praxis Examinations in their teacher education programs at graduate and undergraduate levels, to provide student guidance and allow self-assessment by individual students. The Praxis tests have also been used as comprehensive examinations for undergraduate students and as qualifying exams for graduate students.

Three groups of tests at three different levels of assessment – Praxis I, II and III – constitute the Praxis Examinations. Praxis I measures basic academic skills, Praxis II measures general and subject-specific knowledge and teaching skills, and Praxis III assesses the practical skills demonstrated by the teaching applicant in a required classroom performance.

Praxis I exams are offered in both paper-and-pencil and computer-based formats in nationwide testing centers. Praxis II exams are given in paper-and-pencil format, while Praxis III is conducted in a direct classroom setting.

II. WHAT ARE THE PRAXIS I EXAMINATIONS?

Also described as Pre-Professional Skills Assessments (PPST), the Praxis I measures the candidate's proficiency in the basic academic skills of reading, writing and mathematics.

The PPST Reading and Mathematics test sections consist of 40 multiple-choice questions with 60 minutes of testing time in the paper-and-pencil format, with an additional 38 questions and an essay in the Writing test. The computerized PPST is made up of four separately timed sections – Reading, Mathematics, multiple-choice

Writing and Essay Writing. The testing session for the combined computer-based exam is 4-1/2 hours.

III. WHAT ARE THE PRAXIS II EXAMINATIONS?

Also categorized as Subject Assessments, the Praxis II examinations evaluate the candidate's knowledge of his or her professional area, as well as general and subject-specific teaching skills and knowledge. In addition to Subject Assessments, there are also Principles of Learning and Teaching Tests (PLT) and Teaching Foundations Tests.

The Subject Assessments (Specialty Area Tests) measure general and subject-specific skills and knowledge in a variety of teaching areas. These exams include both multiple-choice and constructed-response items. The PLT tests assess general pedagogical knowledge at four grade levels – Early Childhood, K-6, 5-9, and 7-12. These tests use a case-study approach and feature both kinds of test response items as well. Teaching Foundations Tests assess pedagogy in several areas – Multi-Subject (Elementary), English, Language Arts, Mathematics, Science, and Social Science.

A. What are the Core Battery Examinations?

Core Battery Examinations, still offered in some states, consist of a battery of three (3) discrete tests, which attempt to give a picture of the teacher-candidate's general ability and mental equipment. They are designed to measure the general educational background of college students, not to evaluate advanced preparation. The tests cover three categories: Professional Knowledge, General Knowledge, and Communication and Quantitative Skills. Professional Knowledge includes questions related to the social and cultural forces that influence curriculum and teaching, as well as questions related to general principles of learning and instruction. General Knowledge includes subtests on science and mathematics, social studies, literature and fine arts. Communication Skills measures listening, reading and written English expression and quantitative skills.

B. What are the Content Specialty Examinations?

The Content Specialty Examinations enable the candidate to demonstrate competence in a special field.

C. Which tests should you take?

Candidates for positions in the elementary school area usually take either Elementary Education or Early Childhood Education. Some school systems and colleges, however, require prospective elementary school teachers to take both.

Those who are candidates for secondary school positions customarily take the one Specialty Assessment covering their teaching specialty, although they are also sometimes asked to indicate another specialty – either in secondary education or even in elementary education.

Where school systems require teacher-candidates to take their own examinations in addition to the Praxis, these local exams are usually given at the same time. The school system to which application is made will notify the candidate whether such additional examination is to be given.

The only way to be sure which Praxis you should take is to get this information from the state department of education, the school system, the graduate school or the college to which you plan to have your scores sent.

D. Description of the examinations

The following are brief descriptions of the individual Core Battery and Content Specialty Examinations as drawn from the official bulletin of information for candidates:

## CORE BATTERY EXAMINATIONS

The Core Battery Examinations are designed to appraise your general preparation for teaching. Tests are offered in (1) Professional Knowledge (including questions in Psychological Foundations of Education, Societal Foundations of Education, and Principles of Learning and Teaching), in (2) General Knowledge (including Social Studies, Literature and Fine Arts), and in (3) Communication Skills (Written English Expression). The General Knowledge and Professional Knowledge tests each include four 30-minute sections containing multiple-choice questions or problems. The test of Communication Skills consists of three 30-minute multiple-choice sections and a 30-minute essay. Course work beyond what is required by teacher preparation programs generally is not essential for the General Knowledge tests.

1. Professional Knowledge (Education)

The Professional Knowledge test is designed to provide an indication of the candidate's knowledge and understanding of professional education matters. It contains questions on general principles and methods of teaching, educational psychology and child development, guidance and personnel services, evaluation, principles of curriculum development, and significant research findings in education and related fields.

The test consists of four 30-minute sections, one of which is a pretest section. Each section contains 35 questions. The questions in the pretest section are administered solely for developmental purposes and do not contribute to examinees' scores.

This test assesses the examinee's understanding of the knowledge and skills that a beginning teacher uses in decision making, with emphasis on the context and process of teaching. Questions concerning the process of teaching assess knowledge of appropriate techniques or means of instructional planning, implementation and evaluation, as well as knowledge of what constitutes acceptable professional behavior. Questions concerning the context of teaching assess the examinee's ability to recognize constitutional rights of students and implications for classroom practice; the implications of state, federal and judicial policy; and forces outside the classroom that influence teachers and students. Some questions also assess the examinee's knowledge of activities and functions of professional organizations and of teachers' rights and responsibilities.

2. General Knowledge (Education)

The General Knowledge test assesses the examinee's knowledge and understanding of various disciplines and their interrelationships. The test consists of four separately timed 30-minute sections: Literature and Fine Arts, Mathematics, Science and Social Studies.

*Social Studies, Literature and Fine Arts:* In the modern classroom, the demands made upon the teacher's cultural background extend far beyond any one field of specialization. It is generally agreed that persons entrusted with the education of children need to have a broad perspective on significant factors in contemporary life. The Social Studies, Literature and Fine Arts test is designed to furnish an estimate of the breadth of the candidate's cultural background in these areas rather than mastery of any special subject.

The 30 questions in the Social Studies section of the test assess an understanding of (1) major United States historical and cultural events and movements, political institutions and political values; (2) prominent characteristics of societies and cultures; (3) relationships between culture and individuals; (4) economic concepts and processes; (5) and knowledge of geographical features and characteristics of human settlement and culture; and (6) social science methodologies, methodological tools and data resources.

The 35 questions in the Literature and Fine Arts section of the test are based on passages from literature, photographic reproductions of art works, film stills and photographs of theater or dance performances. The questions using these kinds of materials are designed to assess the examinee's skills in analysis and interpretation.

The *Science and Mathematics* test is designed to furnish an estimate of the candidate's knowledge of important concepts in the fields of science and mathematics, including contemporary developments in these areas.

The 30 questions in the Science section of the test are designed to measure knowledge and understanding of certain themes that are major areas of scientific interest and current concern. Questions selected emphasize important principles, theories, concepts and facts of science; applications of these theories and facts; and the methods of science. The science questions are based on important themes from the biological, physical and earth sciences.

The 25 questions in the Mathematics section of the test are intended to assess the examinee's cumulative knowledge of mathematics. Questions are selected from such topics as comparing and ordering numbers; estimation; interpreting graphs, charts and diagrams; use of ratio, proportion and percent; reading scales; measurement; interpreting formulas and other expressions written in symbols; logical reasoning; and recognition of more than one way to solve a problem.

3. Communication Skills (Written English Expression)

The Communication Skills test is designed to measure the two factors judged to be of particular significance for teachers: general verbal ability and skill in the correct use of the English language. The test contains questions on grammatical usage, punctuation, capitalization, spelling, sentence structure and organization, reading skills, and an essay. The test assesses the examinee's knowledge and skills in the areas of listening, reading and writing.

The Listening section consists of 40 questions that assess the examinee's ability to retain and interpret spoken messages. The questions and the information on which they are based are tape-recorded; they do not appear in the test book. Only the directions and answer choices are printed. Directions are also presented on the tape.

The section is divided into three parts, each with a different question format. In Part A, examinees listen to short statements or questions, then select either the best answer to a question or a sentence that is best supported by the statement. In Part B, examinees listen to short dialogues between two speakers, then answer multiple-choice questions. In Part C, examinees listen to several short talks, each followed by multiple-choice questions.

The Reading section consists of 30 multiple-choice questions that assess the examinee's ability to read for literal content and to analyze and evaluate prose selections. The reading material varies in difficulty and is drawn from a variety of subject areas and real-life situations. The section contains long passages of approximately 250 words, shorter passages of approximately 100 words, and short statements of fewer than 50 words.

The multiple-choice Writing section consists of 45 questions that assess the examinee's ability to use standard written English correctly and effectively and to select and order materials appropriately in sentences or short paragraphs. Examinees are not required to have knowledge of formal grammatical terminology, but rather are asked to detect errors, choose the best way to rewrite certain phrases or sentences, and evaluate strategies for developing ideas.

For the essay component of the Writing section, examinees are asked to write for 30 minutes on an assigned topic. The essays are scored holistically (that is, with a single score for overall quality). Scores are based on such things as the development of the central idea; evidence that the writer understands why the piece is being written and for whom; consistency of point of view; cohesiveness; strength and logic of supporting information; rhetorical force; appropriateness of diction and syntax; and correctness of mechanics and usage.

|  | NLC Book Catalog No. |
|---|---|
| **PRAXIS I: PPST (Pre-Professional Skills Tests)** | |
| PPST Reading | ATS-95 |
| PPST Mathematics | ATS-95 |
| PPST Writing | ATS-95 |
| | |
| **PRAXIS II: NTE Programs Core Battery** | |
| General Knowledge | NC-4, 5, 8 |
| Communication Skills | NC-6 |
| Professional Knowledge | NC-1, 2, 3, 7 |
| | |
| **PRAXIS II: Multiple Subjects Assessment for Teachers (MSAT)** | |
| MSAT: Content Knowledge | NC-9 |
| MSAT: Content Area, Exercises 1 and 2 | NC-9 |
| | |
| **PRAXIS II: Subject Assessments and Content Specialty Tests** | |
| Accounting | NT-51 |
| Agriculture | NT-20 |
| Art Education | NT-13 |
| Audiology | NT-34 |
| Biology and General Science | NT-3 |
| Business Education | NT-10 |
| Chemistry and General Science | NT-7a |
| Chemistry, Physics and General Science | NT-7 |
| Computer Literacy / Data Processing | NT-49 |
| Cooperative Education | NT-52 |
| Dance | NT-66 |
| Early Childhood Education (KG-3) | NT-2 |
| Earth and Space Science | NT-45 |
| Economics | NT-53 |
| Education in an Urban Setting | NT-31 |
| Education in the Elementary School (1-8) | NT-1 |
| Education of the Mentally Retarded | NT-24 |
| Educational Leadership: Administration and Supervision | NT-15 |
| Educational Technology Specialist | NT-67 |
| English as a Second Language | NT-47 |
| English Language and Literature | NT-4 |
| Environmental Education | NT-54 |
| Foreign Language Pedagogy | NT-55 |
| French | NT-19 |
| General Science (Middle School) | NT-48 |
| Geography | NT-56 |
| German | NT-32 |
| Government / Political Science | NT-57 |
| Guidance Counselor | NT-16 |
| Guidance Counselor, Elementary School | NT-16a |
| Guidance Counselor, Junior H.S. | NT-16b |

| | |
|---|---|
| Guidance Counselor, Senior H.S. | NT-16c |
| Health Education | NT-38 |
| Hebrew | NT-68 |
| Home Economics Education (Family Consumer Science) | NT-12 |
| Introduction to the Teaching of Reading | NT-39 |
| Italian | NT-50 |
| Latin | NT-18 |
| Library | NT-17 |
| Literacy | NT-70 |
| Marketing and Distributive Education | NT-46 |
| Mathematics | NT-6 |
| Media Specialist – Library & Audio-Visual Services | NT-29 |
| Men's Physical Education | NT-36 |
| Music Education | NT-11 |
| Office & Secretarial Technology | NT-58 |
| Physical Education | NT-9 |
| Physics and General Science | NT-7b |
| Psychology | NT-42 |
| Reading Specialist | NT-30 |
| Safety / Driver Education | NT-59 |
| School Food Service Supervisor | NT-60 |
| School Psychology | NT-40 |
| School Social Worker | NT-65 |
| Social Studies | NT-8 |
| Sociology | NT-61 |
| Spanish | NT-14 |
| Special Education | NT-41 |
| Speech and Language Pathology | NT-33 |
| Speech Communication | NT-35 |
| Teaching Emotionally Disturbed | NT-43 |
| Teaching Health Conservation | NT-23 |
| Teaching Hearing Handicapped | NT-28 |
| Teaching Learning Disabled | NT-44 |
| Teaching Orthopedically Handicapped | NT-25 |
| Teaching Speech Handicapped | NT-26 |
| Teaching Visually Handicapped | NT-27 |
| Technology (Industrial Arts) Education | NT-5 |
| Theatre | NT-69 |
| Trades and Industrial Education | NT-22 |
| U.S. History | NT-62 |
| Visiting Teacher | NT-21 |
| Vocational General Knowledge | NT-64 |
| Women's Physical Education | NT-37 |
| World Civilization | NT-63 |

## IV. WHAT IS THE PRAXIS III EXAMINATION?

The Praxis III Examination evaluates the candidate's performance in the complex environment of the modern classroom, using the licensing criteria of the state in which the exam is administered.

As the practical section of the Praxis Series, the Praxis III Examination analyzes the candidate's ability to implement his/her ideas in the classroom. This exam includes a training program that utilizes the most recent materials and teaching techniques. The teacher's knowledge of the diverse requirements for different subjects is assessed, as is the candidate's ability to employ the teaching method that is particularly appropriate to the subject being taught.

Trained local observers constitute a qualified committee that examines the teaching applicant's understanding of the specific needs of individual students. Finally, the Praxis III evaluates the candidate's awareness of multi-cultural issues, an important criterion in today's classroom environment.

# SCHOOL FOOD SERVICE SUPERVISOR

The School Food Service Supervisor examination is intended to assess the subject-area competence of persons who are seeking first appointments as school food service supervisors. The test includes questions that assess knowledge of relevant facts and the ability to analyze problems and apply principles. The examination content is appropriate for examinees who have completed the educational requirements for certification as a school food service supervisor.

The School Food Service Supervisor examination tests competence in the two areas and twelve subareas listed below.

I. Nutrition
   A. General Principles:
      Nutrients, food sources, life cycle needs, and contributions to health.
   B. Nutrition Education:
      Implementing dietary guidelines, needs assessment, methods and materials, and evaluation.
   C. Menu Planning:
      Meal patterns, food preferences, and meeting nutritional needs using available resources.

II. Management
   A. Financial:
      Budgeting, recording and reporting, cost control and accountability.
   B. Procurement:
      Bidding and inventory control.
   C. Personnel:
      Legal issues, staff development, and supervision.
   D. Food Production:
      Menu planning, production planning, methods of preparation, quality control, service, and delivery.
   E. Equipment, Layout, and Design:
      Equipment specifications and functions, traffic and product flow, and space allocation.
   F. Safety and Sanitation:
      Safety and sanitation concerns regarding individuals, food, the facility and equipment, and contingency and emergency measures.
   G. Regulations and Standards:
      Reimbursable meals, USDA-donated foods, funding sources, history, and competitive foods.
   H. Communications:
      Marketing, communications with the school and school system, and public relations.
   I. Computers:
      Knowledge of computers and computer applications.

# HOW TO TAKE A TEST

I. YOU MUST PASS AN EXAMINATION

A. *WHAT EVERY CANDIDATE SHOULD KNOW*

Examination applicants often ask us for help in preparing for the written test. What can I study in advance? What kinds of questions will be asked? How will the test be given? How will the papers be graded?

As an applicant for a civil service examination, you may be wondering about some of these things. Our purpose here is to suggest effective methods of advance study and to describe civil service examinations.

Your chances for success on this examination can be increased if you know how to prepare. Those "pre-examination jitters" can be reduced if you know what to expect. You can even experience an adventure in good citizenship if you know why civil service exams are given.

B. *WHY ARE CIVIL SERVICE EXAMINATIONS GIVEN?*

Civil service examinations are important to you in two ways. As a citizen, you want public jobs filled by employees who know how to do their work. As a job seeker, you want a fair chance to compete for that job on an equal footing with other candidates. The best-known means of accomplishing this two-fold goal is the competitive examination.

Exams are widely publicized throughout the nation. They may be administered for jobs in federal, state, city, municipal, town or village governments or agencies.

Any citizen may apply, with some limitations, such as the age or residence of applicants. Your experience and education may be reviewed to see whether you meet the requirements for the particular examination. When these requirements exist, they are reasonable and applied consistently to all applicants. Thus, a competitive examination may cause you some uneasiness now, but it is your privilege and safeguard.

C. *HOW ARE CIVIL SERVICE EXAMS DEVELOPED?*

Examinations are carefully written by trained technicians who are specialists in the field known as "psychological measurement," in consultation with recognized authorities in the field of work that the test will cover. These experts recommend the subject matter areas or skills to be tested; only those knowledges or skills important to your success on the job are included. The most reliable books and source materials available are used as references. Together, the experts and technicians judge the difficulty level of the questions.

Test technicians know how to phrase questions so that the problem is clearly stated. Their ethics do not permit "trick" or "catch" questions. Questions may have been tried out on sample groups, or subjected to statistical analysis, to determine their usefulness.

Written tests are often used in combination with performance tests, ratings of training and experience, and oral interviews. All of these measures combine to form the best-known means of finding the right person for the right job.

## II. HOW TO PASS THE WRITTEN TEST

### A. NATURE OF THE EXAMINATION

To prepare intelligently for civil service examinations, you should know how they differ from school examinations you have taken. In school you were assigned certain definite pages to read or subjects to cover. The examination questions were quite detailed and usually emphasized memory. Civil service exams, on the other hand, try to discover your present ability to perform the duties of a position, plus your potentiality to learn these duties. In other words, a civil service exam attempts to predict how successful you will be. Questions cover such a broad area that they cannot be as minute and detailed as school exam questions.

In the public service similar kinds of work, or positions, are grouped together in one "class." This process is known as *position-classification*. All the positions in a class are paid according to the salary range for that class. One class title covers all of these positions, and they are all tested by the same examination.

### B. FOUR BASIC STEPS

#### 1) Study the announcement

How, then, can you know what subjects to study? Our best answer is: "Learn as much as possible about the class of positions for which you've applied." The exam will test the knowledge, skills and abilities needed to do the work.

Your most valuable source of information about the position you want is the official exam announcement. This announcement lists the training and experience qualifications. Check these standards and apply only if you come reasonably close to meeting them.

The brief description of the position in the examination announcement offers some clues to the subjects which will be tested. Think about the job itself. Review the duties in your mind. Can you perform them, or are there some in which you are rusty? Fill in the blank spots in your preparation.

Many jurisdictions preview the written test in the exam announcement by including a section called "Knowledge and Abilities Required," "Scope of the Examination," or some similar heading. Here you will find out specifically what fields will be tested.

#### 2) Review your own background

Once you learn in general what the position is all about, and what you need to know to do the work, ask yourself which subjects you already know fairly well and which need improvement. You may wonder whether to concentrate on improving your strong areas or on building some background in your fields of weakness. When the announcement has specified "some knowledge" or "considerable knowledge," or has used adjectives like "beginning principles of…" or "advanced … methods," you can get a clue as to the number and difficulty of questions to be asked in any given field. More questions, and hence broader coverage, would be included for those subjects which are more important in the work. Now weigh your strengths and weaknesses against the job requirements and prepare accordingly.

#### 3) Determine the level of the position

Another way to tell how intensively you should prepare is to understand the level of the job for which you are applying. Is it the entering level? In other words, is this the position in which beginners in a field of work are hired? Or is it an intermediate or advanced level? Sometimes this is indicated by such words as "Junior" or "Senior" in the class title. Other jurisdictions use Roman numerals to designate the level – Clerk I, Clerk II, for example. The word "Supervisor" sometimes appears in the title. If the level is not indicated by the title, check the description of duties. Will you be working under very close supervision, or will you have responsibility for independent decisions in this work?

### 4) Choose appropriate study materials

Now that you know the subjects to be examined and the relative amount of each subject to be covered, you can choose suitable study materials. For beginning level jobs, or even advanced ones, if you have a pronounced weakness in some aspect of your training, read a modern, standard textbook in that field. Be sure it is up to date and has general coverage. Such books are normally available at your library, and the librarian will be glad to help you locate one. For entry-level positions, questions of appropriate difficulty are chosen – neither highly advanced questions, nor those too simple. Such questions require careful thought but not advanced training.

If the position for which you are applying is technical or advanced, you will read more advanced, specialized material. If you are already familiar with the basic principles of your field, elementary textbooks would waste your time. Concentrate on advanced textbooks and technical periodicals. Think through the concepts and review difficult problems in your field.

These are all general sources. You can get more ideas on your own initiative, following these leads. For example, training manuals and publications of the government agency which employs workers in your field can be useful, particularly for technical and professional positions. A letter or visit to the government department involved may result in more specific study suggestions, and certainly will provide you with a more definite idea of the exact nature of the position you are seeking.


## III. KINDS OF TESTS

Tests are used for purposes other than measuring knowledge and ability to perform specified duties. For some positions, it is equally important to test ability to make adjustments to new situations or to profit from training. In others, basic mental abilities not dependent on information are essential. Questions which test these things may not appear as pertinent to the duties of the position as those which test for knowledge and information. Yet they are often highly important parts of a fair examination. For very general questions, it is almost impossible to help you direct your study efforts. What we can do is to point out some of the more common of these general abilities needed in public service positions and describe some typical questions.

1) General information

Broad, general information has been found useful for predicting job success in some kinds of work. This is tested in a variety of ways, from vocabulary lists to questions about current events. Basic background in some field of work, such as sociology or economics, may be sampled in a group of questions. Often these are principles which have become familiar to most persons through exposure rather than through formal training. It is difficult to advise you how to study for these questions; being alert to the world around you is our best suggestion.

2) Verbal ability

An example of an ability needed in many positions is verbal or language ability. Verbal ability is, in brief, the ability to use and understand words. Vocabulary and grammar tests are typical measures of this ability. Reading comprehension or paragraph interpretation questions are common in many kinds of civil service tests. You are given a paragraph of written material and asked to find its central meaning.

3) Numerical ability

Number skills can be tested by the familiar arithmetic problem, by checking paired lists of numbers to see which are alike and which are different, or by interpreting charts and graphs. In the latter test, a graph may be printed in the test booklet which you are asked to use as the basis for answering questions.

4) Observation

A popular test for law-enforcement positions is the observation test. A picture is shown to you for several minutes, then taken away. Questions about the picture test your ability to observe both details and larger elements.

5) Following directions

In many positions in the public service, the employee must be able to carry out written instructions dependably and accurately. You may be given a chart with several columns, each column listing a variety of information. The questions require you to carry out directions involving the information given in the chart.

6) Skills and aptitudes

Performance tests effectively measure some manual skills and aptitudes. When the skill is one in which you are trained, such as typing or shorthand, you can practice. These tests are often very much like those given in business school or high school courses. For many of the other skills and aptitudes, however, no short-time preparation can be made. Skills and abilities natural to you or that you have developed throughout your lifetime are being tested.

Many of the general questions just described provide all the data needed to answer the questions and ask you to use your reasoning ability to find the answers. Your best preparation for these tests, as well as for tests of facts and ideas, is to be at your physical and mental best. You, no doubt, have your own methods of getting into an exam-taking mood and keeping "in shape." The next section lists some ideas on this subject.


IV. KINDS OF QUESTIONS

Only rarely is the "essay" question, which you answer in narrative form, used in civil service tests. Civil service tests are usually of the short-answer type. Full instructions for answering these questions will be given to you at the examination. But in case this is your first experience with short-answer questions and separate answer sheets, here is what you need to know:

**1) Multiple-choice Questions**

Most popular of the short-answer questions is the "multiple choice" or "best answer" question. It can be used, for example, to test for factual knowledge, ability to solve problems or judgment in meeting situations found at work.

A multiple-choice question is normally one of three types—
- It can begin with an incomplete statement followed by several possible endings. You are to find the one ending which *best* completes the statement, although some of the others may not be entirely wrong.
- It can also be a complete statement in the form of a question which is answered by choosing one of the statements listed.

- It can be in the form of a problem – again you select the best answer.

Here is an example of a multiple-choice question with a discussion which should give you some clues as to the method for choosing the right answer:

When an employee has a complaint about his assignment, the action which will *best* help him overcome his difficulty is to
    A. discuss his difficulty with his coworkers
    B. take the problem to the head of the organization
    C. take the problem to the person who gave him the assignment
    D. say nothing to anyone about his complaint

In answering this question, you should study each of the choices to find which is best. Consider choice "A" – Certainly an employee may discuss his complaint with fellow employees, but no change or improvement can result, and the complaint remains unresolved. Choice "B" is a poor choice since the head of the organization probably does not know what assignment you have been given, and taking your problem to him is known as "going over the head" of the supervisor. The supervisor, or person who made the assignment, is the person who can clarify it or correct any injustice. Choice "C" is, therefore, correct. To say nothing, as in choice "D," is unwise. Supervisors have and interest in knowing the problems employees are facing, and the employee is seeking a solution to his problem.

## 2) True/False Questions

The "true/false" or "right/wrong" form of question is sometimes used. Here a complete statement is given. Your job is to decide whether the statement is right or wrong.

SAMPLE: A roaming cell-phone call to a nearby city costs less than a non-roaming call to a distant city.

This statement is wrong, or false, since roaming calls are more expensive.

This is not a complete list of all possible question forms, although most of the others are variations of these common types. You will always get complete directions for answering questions. Be sure you understand *how* to mark your answers – ask questions until you do.


## V. RECORDING YOUR ANSWERS

Computer terminals are used more and more today for many different kinds of exams.

For an examination with very few applicants, you may be told to record your answers in the test booklet itself. Separate answer sheets are much more common. If this separate answer sheet is to be scored by machine – and this is often the case – it is highly important that you mark your answers correctly in order to get credit.

An electronic scoring machine is often used in civil service offices because of the speed with which papers can be scored. Machine-scored answer sheets must be marked with a pencil, which will be given to you. This pencil has a high graphite content which responds to the electronic scoring machine. As a matter of fact, stray dots may register as answers, so do not let your pencil rest on the answer sheet while you are pondering the correct answer. Also, if your pencil lead breaks or is otherwise defective, ask for another.

Since the answer sheet will be dropped in a slot in the scoring machine, be careful not to bend the corners or get the paper crumpled.

The answer sheet normally has five vertical columns of numbers, with 30 numbers to a column. These numbers correspond to the question numbers in your test booklet. After each number, going across the page are four or five pairs of dotted lines. These short dotted lines have small letters or numbers above them. The first two pairs may also have a "T" or "F" above the letters. This indicates that the first two pairs only are to be used if the questions are of the true-false type. If the questions are multiple choice, disregard the "T" and "F" and pay attention only to the small letters or numbers.

Answer your questions in the manner of the sample that follows:

32. The largest city in the United States is
    A. Washington, D.C.
    B. New York City
    C. Chicago
    D. Detroit
    E. San Francisco

1) Choose the answer you think is best. (New York City is the largest, so "B" is correct.)
2) Find the row of dotted lines numbered the same as the question you are answering. (Find row number 32)
3) Find the pair of dotted lines corresponding to the answer. (Find the pair of lines under the mark "B.")
4) Make a solid black mark between the dotted lines.


## VI. BEFORE THE TEST

Common sense will help you find procedures to follow to get ready for an examination. Too many of us, however, overlook these sensible measures. Indeed, nervousness and fatigue have been found to be the most serious reasons why applicants fail to do their best on civil service tests. Here is a list of reminders:

- Begin your preparation early – Don't wait until the last minute to go scurrying around for books and materials or to find out what the position is all about.
- Prepare continuously – An hour a night for a week is better than an all-night cram session. This has been definitely established. What is more, a night a week for a month will return better dividends than crowding your study into a shorter period of time.
- Locate the place of the exam – You have been sent a notice telling you when and where to report for the examination. If the location is in a different town or otherwise unfamiliar to you, it would be well to inquire the best route and learn something about the building.
- Relax the night before the test – Allow your mind to rest. Do not study at all that night. Plan some mild recreation or diversion; then go to bed early and get a good night's sleep.
- Get up early enough to make a leisurely trip to the place for the test – This way unforeseen events, traffic snarls, unfamiliar buildings, etc. will not upset you.
- Dress comfortably – A written test is not a fashion show. You will be known by number and not by name, so wear something comfortable.

- Leave excess paraphernalia at home – Shopping bags and odd bundles will get in your way. You need bring only the items mentioned in the official notice you received; usually everything you need is provided. Do not bring reference books to the exam. They will only confuse those last minutes and be taken away from you when in the test room.
- Arrive somewhat ahead of time – If because of transportation schedules you must get there very early, bring a newspaper or magazine to take your mind off yourself while waiting.
- Locate the examination room – When you have found the proper room, you will be directed to the seat or part of the room where you will sit. Sometimes you are given a sheet of instructions to read while you are waiting. Do not fill out any forms until you are told to do so; just read them and be prepared.
- Relax and prepare to listen to the instructions
- If you have any physical problem that may keep you from doing your best, be sure to tell the test administrator. If you are sick or in poor health, you really cannot do your best on the exam. You can come back and take the test some other time.

## VII. AT THE TEST

The day of the test is here and you have the test booklet in your hand. The temptation to get going is very strong. Caution! There is more to success than knowing the right answers. You must know how to identify your papers and understand variations in the type of short-answer question used in this particular examination. Follow these suggestions for maximum results from your efforts:

### 1) Cooperate with the monitor

The test administrator has a duty to create a situation in which you can be as much at ease as possible. He will give instructions, tell you when to begin, check to see that you are marking your answer sheet correctly, and so on. He is not there to guard you, although he will see that your competitors do not take unfair advantage. He wants to help you do your best.

### 2) Listen to all instructions

Don't jump the gun! Wait until you understand all directions. In most civil service tests you get more time than you need to answer the questions. So don't be in a hurry. Read each word of instructions until you clearly understand the meaning. Study the examples, listen to all announcements and follow directions. Ask questions if you do not understand what to do.

### 3) Identify your papers

Civil service exams are usually identified by number only. You will be assigned a number; you must not put your name on your test papers. Be sure to copy your number correctly. Since more than one exam may be given, copy your exact examination title.

### 4) Plan your time

Unless you are told that a test is a "speed" or "rate of work" test, speed itself is usually not important. Time enough to answer all the questions will be provided, but this does not mean that you have all day. An overall time limit has been set. Divide the total time (in minutes) by the number of questions to determine the approximate time you have for each question.

### 5) Do not linger over difficult questions

If you come across a difficult question, mark it with a paper clip (useful to have along) and come back to it when you have been through the booklet. One caution if you do this – be sure to skip a number on your answer sheet as well. Check often to be sure that you have not lost your place and that you are marking in the row numbered the same as the question you are answering.

### 6) Read the questions

Be sure you know what the question asks! Many capable people are unsuccessful because they failed to *read* the questions correctly.

### 7) Answer all questions

Unless you have been instructed that a penalty will be deducted for incorrect answers, it is better to guess than to omit a question.

### 8) Speed tests

It is often better NOT to guess on speed tests. It has been found that on timed tests people are tempted to spend the last few seconds before time is called in marking answers at random – without even reading them – in the hope of picking up a few extra points. To discourage this practice, the instructions may warn you that your score will be "corrected" for guessing. That is, a penalty will be applied. The incorrect answers will be deducted from the correct ones, or some other penalty formula will be used.

### 9) Review your answers

If you finish before time is called, go back to the questions you guessed or omitted to give them further thought. Review other answers if you have time.

### 10) Return your test materials

If you are ready to leave before others have finished or time is called, take ALL your materials to the monitor and leave quietly. Never take any test material with you. The monitor can discover whose papers are not complete, and taking a test booklet may be grounds for disqualification.

## VIII. EXAMINATION TECHNIQUES

1) Read the general instructions carefully. These are usually printed on the first page of the exam booklet. As a rule, these instructions refer to the timing of the examination; the fact that you should not start work until the signal and must stop work at a signal, etc. If there are any *special* instructions, such as a choice of questions to be answered, make sure that you note this instruction carefully.

2) When you are ready to start work on the examination, that is as soon as the signal has been given, read the instructions to each question booklet, underline any key words or phrases, such as *least, best, outline, describe* and the like. In this way you will tend to answer as requested rather than discover on reviewing your paper that you *listed without describing*, that you selected the *worst* choice rather than the *best* choice, etc.

3) If the examination is of the objective or multiple-choice type – that is, each question will also give a series of possible answers: A, B, C or D, and you are called upon to select the best answer and write the letter next to that answer on your answer paper – it is advisable to start answering each question in turn. There may be anywhere from 50 to 100 such questions in the three or four hours allotted and you can see how much time would be taken if you read through all the questions before beginning to answer any. Furthermore, if you come across a question or group of questions which you know would be difficult to answer, it would undoubtedly affect your handling of all the other questions.

4) If the examination is of the essay type and contains but a few questions, it is a moot point as to whether you should read all the questions before starting to answer any one. Of course, if you are given a choice – say five out of seven and the like – then it is essential to read all the questions so you can eliminate the two that are most difficult. If, however, you are asked to answer all the questions, there may be danger in trying to answer the easiest one first because you may find that you will spend too much time on it. The best technique is to answer the first question, then proceed to the second, etc.

5) Time your answers. Before the exam begins, write down the time it started, then add the time allowed for the examination and write down the time it must be completed, then divide the time available somewhat as follows:
   - If 3-1/2 hours are allowed, that would be 210 minutes. If you have 80 objective-type questions, that would be an average of 2-1/2 minutes per question. Allow yourself no more than 2 minutes per question, or a total of 160 minutes, which will permit about 50 minutes to review.
   - If for the time allotment of 210 minutes there are 7 essay questions to answer, that would average about 30 minutes a question. Give yourself only 25 minutes per question so that you have about 35 minutes to review.

6) The most important instruction is to *read each question* and make sure you know what is wanted. The second most important instruction is to *time yourself properly* so that you answer every question. The third most Important instruction is to *answer every question*. Guess if you have to but include something for each question. Remember that you will receive no credit for a blank and will probably receive some credit if you write something in answer to an essay question. If you guess a letter – say "B" for a multiple-choice question – you may have guessed right. If you leave a blank as an answer to a multiple-choice question, the examiners may respect your feelings but it will not add a point to your score. Some exams may penalize you for wrong answers, so in such cases *only*, you may not want to guess unless you have some basis for your answer.

7) Suggestions
   a. Objective-type questions
      1. Examine the question booklet for proper sequence of pages and questions
      2. Read all instructions carefully
      3. Skip any question which seems too difficult; return to it after all other questions have been answered
      4. Apportion your time properly; do not spend too much time on any single question or group of questions

5. Note and underline key words – *all, most, fewest, least, best, worst, same, opposite,* etc.
6. Pay particular attention to negatives
7. Note unusual option, e.g., unduly long, short, complex, different or similar in content to the body of the question
8. Observe the use of "hedging" words – *probably, may, most likely,* etc.
9. Make sure that your answer is put next to the same number as the question
10. Do not second-guess unless you have good reason to believe the second answer is definitely more correct
11. Cross out original answer if you decide another answer is more accurate; do not erase until you are ready to hand your paper in
12. Answer all questions; guess unless instructed otherwise
13. Leave time for review

  b. Essay questions
    1. Read each question carefully
    2. Determine exactly what is wanted. Underline key words or phrases.
    3. Decide on outline or paragraph answer
    4. Include many different points and elements unless asked to develop any one or two points or elements
    5. Show impartiality by giving pros and cons unless directed to select one side only
    6. Make and write down any assumptions you find necessary to answer the questions
    7. Watch your English, grammar, punctuation and choice of words
    8. Time your answers; don't crowd material

8) Answering the essay question

Most essay questions can be answered by framing the specific response around several key words or ideas. Here are a few such key words or ideas:

M's: manpower, materials, methods, money, management
P's: purpose, program, policy, plan, procedure, practice, problems, pitfalls, personnel, public relations
  a. Six basic steps in handling problems:
    1. Preliminary plan and background development
    2. Collect information, data and facts
    3. Analyze and interpret information, data and facts
    4. Analyze and develop solutions as well as make recommendations
    5. Prepare report and sell recommendations
    6. Install recommendations and follow up effectiveness

  b. Pitfalls to avoid
    1. *Taking things for granted* – A statement of the situation does not necessarily imply that each of the elements is necessarily true; for example, a complaint may be invalid and biased so that all that can be taken for granted is that a complaint has been registered

2. *Considering only one side of a situation* – Wherever possible, indicate several alternatives and then point out the reasons you selected the best one
3. *Failing to indicate follow up* – Whenever your answer indicates action on your part, make certain that you will take proper follow-up action to see how successful your recommendations, procedures or actions turn out to be
4. *Taking too long in answering any single question* – Remember to time your answers properly

## IX. AFTER THE TEST

Scoring procedures differ in detail among civil service jurisdictions although the general principles are the same. Whether the papers are hand-scored or graded by machine we have described, they are nearly always graded by number. That is, the person who marks the paper knows only the number – never the name – of the applicant. Not until all the papers have been graded will they be matched with names. If other tests, such as training and experience or oral interview ratings have been given, scores will be combined. Different parts of the examination usually have different weights. For example, the written test might count 60 percent of the final grade, and a rating of training and experience 40 percent. In many jurisdictions, veterans will have a certain number of points added to their grades.

After the final grade has been determined, the names are placed in grade order and an eligible list is established. There are various methods for resolving ties between those who get the same final grade – probably the most common is to place first the name of the person whose application was received first. Job offers are made from the eligible list in the order the names appear on it. You will be notified of your grade and your rank as soon as all these computations have been made. This will be done as rapidly as possible.

People who are found to meet the requirements in the announcement are called "eligibles." Their names are put on a list of eligible candidates. An eligible's chances of getting a job depend on how high he stands on this list and how fast agencies are filling jobs from the list.

When a job is to be filled from a list of eligibles, the agency asks for the names of people on the list of eligibles for that job. When the civil service commission receives this request, it sends to the agency the names of the three people highest on this list. Or, if the job to be filled has specialized requirements, the office sends the agency the names of the top three persons who meet these requirements from the general list.

The appointing officer makes a choice from among the three people whose names were sent to him. If the selected person accepts the appointment, the names of the others are put back on the list to be considered for future openings.

That is the rule in hiring from all kinds of eligible lists, whether they are for typist, carpenter, chemist, or something else. For every vacancy, the appointing officer has his choice of any one of the top three eligibles on the list. This explains why the person whose name is on top of the list sometimes does not get an appointment when some of the persons lower on the list do. If the appointing officer chooses the second or third eligible, the No. 1 eligible does not get a job at once, but stays on the list until he is appointed or the list is terminated.

## X. HOW TO PASS THE INTERVIEW TEST

The examination for which you applied requires an oral interview test. You have already taken the written test and you are now being called for the interview test – the final part of the formal examination.

You may think that it is not possible to prepare for an interview test and that there are no procedures to follow during an interview. Our purpose is to point out some things you can do in advance that will help you and some good rules to follow and pitfalls to avoid while you are being interviewed.

*What is an interview supposed to test?*

The written examination is designed to test the technical knowledge and competence of the candidate; the oral is designed to evaluate intangible qualities, not readily measured otherwise, and to establish a list showing the relative fitness of each candidate – as measured against his competitors – for the position sought. Scoring is not on the basis of "right" and "wrong," but on a sliding scale of values ranging from "not passable" to "outstanding." As a matter of fact, it is possible to achieve a relatively low score without a single "incorrect" answer because of evident weakness in the qualities being measured.

Occasionally, an examination may consist entirely of an oral test – either an individual or a group oral. In such cases, information is sought concerning the technical knowledges and abilities of the candidate, since there has been no written examination for this purpose. More commonly, however, an oral test is used to supplement a written examination.

*Who conducts interviews?*

The composition of oral boards varies among different jurisdictions. In nearly all, a representative of the personnel department serves as chairman. One of the members of the board may be a representative of the department in which the candidate would work. In some cases, "outside experts" are used, and, frequently, a businessman or some other representative of the general public is asked to serve. Labor and management or other special groups may be represented. The aim is to secure the services of experts in the appropriate field.

However the board is composed, it is a good idea (and not at all improper or unethical) to ascertain in advance of the interview who the members are and what groups they represent. When you are introduced to them, you will have some idea of their backgrounds and interests, and at least you will not stutter and stammer over their names.

*What should be done before the interview?*

While knowledge about the board members is useful and takes some of the surprise element out of the interview, there is other preparation which is more substantive. It *is* possible to prepare for an oral interview – in several ways:

**1) Keep a copy of your application and review it carefully before the interview**

This may be the only document before the oral board, and the starting point of the interview. Know what education and experience you have listed there, and the sequence and dates of all of it. Sometimes the board will ask you to review the highlights of your experience for them; you should not have to hem and haw doing it.

**2) Study the class specification and the examination announcement**

Usually, the oral board has one or both of these to guide them. The qualities, characteristics or knowledges required by the position sought are stated in these documents. They offer valuable clues as to the nature of the oral interview. For example, if the job involves supervisory responsibilities, the announcement will usually indicate that knowledge of modern supervisory methods and the qualifications of the candidate as a supervisor will be tested. If so, you can expect such questions, frequently in the form of a hypothetical situation which you are expected to solve. NEVER go into an oral without knowledge of the duties and responsibilities of the job you seek.

**3) Think through each qualification required**

Try to visualize the kind of questions you would ask if you were a board member. How well could you answer them? Try especially to appraise your own knowledge and background in each area, *measured against the job sought*, and identify any areas in which you are weak. Be critical and realistic – do not flatter yourself.

**4) Do some general reading in areas in which you feel you may be weak**

For example, if the job involves supervision and your past experience has NOT, some general reading in supervisory methods and practices, particularly in the field of human relations, might be useful. Do NOT study agency procedures or detailed manuals. The oral board will be testing your understanding and capacity, not your memory.

**5) Get a good night's sleep and watch your general health and mental attitude**

You will want a clear head at the interview. Take care of a cold or any other minor ailment, and of course, no hangovers.

*What should be done on the day of the interview?*

Now comes the day of the interview itself. Give yourself plenty of time to get there. Plan to arrive somewhat ahead of the scheduled time, particularly if your appointment is in the fore part of the day. If a previous candidate fails to appear, the board might be ready for you a bit early. By early afternoon an oral board is almost invariably behind schedule if there are many candidates, and you may have to wait. Take along a book or magazine to read, or your application to review, but leave any extraneous material in the waiting room when you go in for your interview. In any event, relax and compose yourself.

The matter of dress is important. The board is forming impressions about you – from your experience, your manners, your attitude, and your appearance. Give your personal appearance careful attention. Dress your best, but not your flashiest. Choose conservative, appropriate clothing, and be sure it is immaculate. This is a business interview, and your appearance should indicate that you regard it as such. Besides, being well groomed and properly dressed will help boost your confidence.

Sooner or later, someone will call your name and escort you into the interview room. *This is it.* From here on you are on your own. It is too late for any more preparation. But remember, you asked for this opportunity to prove your fitness, and you are here because your request was granted.

*What happens when you go in?*

The usual sequence of events will be as follows: The clerk (who is often the board stenographer) will introduce you to the chairman of the oral board, who will introduce you to the other members of the board. Acknowledge the introductions before you sit down. Do not be surprised if you find a microphone facing you or a stenotypist sitting by. Oral interviews are usually recorded in the event of an appeal or other review.

Usually the chairman of the board will open the interview by reviewing the highlights of your education and work experience from your application – primarily for the benefit of the other members of the board, as well as to get the material into the record. Do not interrupt or comment unless there is an error or significant misinterpretation; if that is the case, do not hesitate. But do not quibble about insignificant matters. Also, he will usually ask you some question about your education, experience or your present job – partly to get you to start talking and to establish the interviewing "rapport." He may start the actual questioning, or turn it over to one of the other members. Frequently, each member undertakes the questioning on a particular area, one in which he is perhaps most competent, so you can expect each member to participate in the examination. Because time is limited, you may also expect some rather abrupt switches in the direction the questioning takes, so do not be upset by it. Normally, a board member will not pursue a single line of questioning unless he discovers a particular strength or weakness.

After each member has participated, the chairman will usually ask whether any member has any further questions, then will ask you if you have anything you wish to add. Unless you are expecting this question, it may floor you. Worse, it may start you off on an extended, extemporaneous speech. The board is not usually seeking more information. The question is principally to offer you a last opportunity to present further qualifications or to indicate that you have nothing to add. So, if you feel that a significant qualification or characteristic has been overlooked, it is proper to point it out in a sentence or so. Do not compliment the board on the thoroughness of their examination – they have been sketchy, and you know it. If you wish, merely say, "No thank you, I have nothing further to add." This is a point where you can "talk yourself out" of a good impression or fail to present an important bit of information. Remember, *you close the interview yourself*.

The chairman will then say, "That is all, Mr. _____, thank you." Do not be startled; the interview is over, and quicker than you think. Thank him, gather your belongings and take your leave. Save your sigh of relief for the other side of the door.

*How to put your best foot forward*

Throughout this entire process, you may feel that the board individually and collectively is trying to pierce your defenses, seek out your hidden weaknesses and embarrass and confuse you. Actually, this is not true. They are obliged to make an appraisal of your qualifications for the job you are seeking, and they want to see you in your best light. Remember, they must interview all candidates and a non-cooperative candidate may become a failure in spite of their best efforts to bring out his qualifications. Here are 15 suggestions that will help you:

1) **Be natural – Keep your attitude confident, not cocky**

If you are not confident that you can do the job, do not expect the board to be. Do not apologize for your weaknesses, try to bring out your strong points. The board is interested in a positive, not negative, presentation. Cockiness will antagonize any board member and make him wonder if you are covering up a weakness by a false show of strength.

2) **Get comfortable, but don't lounge or sprawl**

Sit erectly but not stiffly. A careless posture may lead the board to conclude that you are careless in other things, or at least that you are not impressed by the importance of the occasion. Either conclusion is natural, even if incorrect. Do not fuss with your clothing, a pencil or an ashtray. Your hands may occasionally be useful to emphasize a point; do not let them become a point of distraction.

3) **Do not wisecrack or make small talk**

This is a serious situation, and your attitude should show that you consider it as such. Further, the time of the board is limited – they do not want to waste it, and neither should you.

### 4) Do not exaggerate your experience or abilities

In the first place, from information in the application or other interviews and sources, the board may know more about you than you think. Secondly, you probably will not get away with it. An experienced board is rather adept at spotting such a situation, so do not take the chance.

### 5) If you know a board member, do not make a point of it, yet do not hide it

Certainly you are not fooling him, and probably not the other members of the board. Do not try to take advantage of your acquaintanceship – it will probably do you little good.

### 6) Do not dominate the interview

Let the board do that. They will give you the clues – do not assume that you have to do all the talking. Realize that the board has a number of questions to ask you, and do not try to take up all the interview time by showing off your extensive knowledge of the answer to the first one.

### 7) Be attentive

You only have 20 minutes or so, and you should keep your attention at its sharpest throughout. When a member is addressing a problem or question to you, give him your undivided attention. Address your reply principally to him, but do not exclude the other board members.

### 8) Do not interrupt

A board member may be stating a problem for you to analyze. He will ask you a question when the time comes. Let him state the problem, and wait for the question.

### 9) Make sure you understand the question

Do not try to answer until you are sure what the question is. If it is not clear, restate it in your own words or ask the board member to clarify it for you. However, do not haggle about minor elements.

### 10) Reply promptly but not hastily

A common entry on oral board rating sheets is "candidate responded readily," or "candidate hesitated in replies." Respond as promptly and quickly as you can, but do not jump to a hasty, ill-considered answer.

### 11) Do not be peremptory in your answers

A brief answer is proper – but do not fire your answer back. That is a losing game from your point of view. The board member can probably ask questions much faster than you can answer them.

### 12) Do not try to create the answer you think the board member wants

He is interested in what kind of mind you have and how it works – not in playing games. Furthermore, he can usually spot this practice and will actually grade you down on it.

### 13) Do not switch sides in your reply merely to agree with a board member

Frequently, a member will take a contrary position merely to draw you out and to see if you are willing and able to defend your point of view. Do not start a debate, yet do not surrender a good position. If a position is worth taking, it is worth defending.

### 14) Do not be afraid to admit an error in judgment if you are shown to be wrong

The board knows that you are forced to reply without any opportunity for careful consideration. Your answer may be demonstrably wrong. If so, admit it and get on with the interview.

### 15) Do not dwell at length on your present job

The opening question may relate to your present assignment. Answer the question but do not go into an extended discussion. You are being examined for a *new* job, not your present one. As a matter of fact, try to phrase ALL your answers in terms of the job for which you are being examined.

*Basis of Rating*

Probably you will forget most of these "do's" and "don'ts" when you walk into the oral interview room. Even remembering them all will not ensure you a passing grade. Perhaps you did not have the qualifications in the first place. But remembering them will help you to put your best foot forward, without treading on the toes of the board members.

Rumor and popular opinion to the contrary notwithstanding, an oral board wants you to make the best appearance possible. They know you are under pressure – but they also want to see how you respond to it as a guide to what your reaction would be under the pressures of the job you seek. They will be influenced by the degree of poise you display, the personal traits you show and the manner in which you respond.

## ABOUT THIS BOOK

This book contains tests divided into Examination Sections. Go through each test, answering every question in the margin. We have also attached a sample answer sheet at the back of the book that can be removed and used. At the end of each test look at the answer key and check your answers. On the ones you got wrong, look at the right answer choice and learn. Do not fill in the answers first. Do not memorize the questions and answers, but understand the answer and principles involved. On your test, the questions will likely be different from the samples. Questions are changed and new ones added. If you understand these past questions you should have success with any changes that arise. Tests may consist of several types of questions. We have additional books on each subject should more study be advisable or necessary for you. Finally, the more you study, the better prepared you will be. This book is intended to be the last thing you study before you walk into the examination room. Prior study of relevant texts is also recommended. NLC publishes some of these in our Fundamental Series. Knowledge and good sense are important factors in passing your exam. Good luck also helps. So now study this Passbook, absorb the material contained within and take that knowledge into the examination. Then do your best to pass that exam.

# EXAMINATION SECTION

# EXAMINATION SECTION
## TEST 1

DIRECTIONS: Each question or incomplete statement is followed by several suggested answers or completions. Select the one that BEST answers the question or completes the statement. *PRINT THE LETTER OF THE CORRECT ANSWER IN THE SPACE AT THE RIGHT.*

1. The one of the following entrees which offers the LEAST variation in texture is    1._____

    A. turkey, cranberry sauce, fried golden brown potatoes, peas
    B. chopped sirloin, mushroom gravy, French fried potatoes broccoli spears
    C. oven-fried chicken, baked potato, peas and carrots, salad
    D. meat loaf, mashed potatoes, creamed spinach, white bread

2. In planning a menu, the FIRST item which should be chosen is the    2._____

    A. vegetable    B. salad    C. entree    D. dessert

3. Of the following, the BEST method of tenderizing cuts of meat which are less tender is by    3._____

    A. broiling    B. stewing    C. baking    D. deep-frying

4. Which one of the following statements regarding proteins is CORRECT?    4._____

    A. The amount of protein in the body is a constant.
    B. The presence of nitrogen distinguishes protein from carbohydrates and fat.
    C. Protein provides more calories per gram than carbohydrates or fat.
    D. Protein provides the principal source of glucose to brain tissue.

5. The one of the following foods that provides MORE vitamin C per serving than the others is    5._____

    A. brussels sprouts    B. cabbage
    C. tomatoes    D. turnips

6. Liver is a PRIMARY source of which one of the following vitamins?    6._____

    A. A    B. $B_6$    C. C    D. D

7. Vitamin A is a fat soluble vitamin essential in an adequate diet for children and adults. Which one of the following statements concerning vitamin A is TRUE?    7._____

    A. The Recommended Daily Allowance for vitamin A for the adult male and female 10 years of age and older is the same.
    B. The Recommended Daily Allowance for vitamin A is expressed in terms of U.S.P. units.
    C. Vegetables have vitamin A activity equal to vitamin A in animal foods.
    D. Excessive amounts of vitamin A are well tolerated by adults.

8. Iron is a mineral required for growth and to keep the body functioning properly. Of the following, the combination of foods that will provide the BEST intake of iron is    8._____

    A. green peas, liver, enriched bread, dried potatoes
    B. cheese, oranges, liver, butter

C. peanut butter, milk, carrots, liver
D. liver, ice cream, chicken, peaches

9. Calcium and phosphorous account for approximately three-fourths of the mineral elements in the body. Their intake is important for adequate nutrition.
Which one of the following statements is CORRECT about both minerals?

   A. For children and young adults, the Recommended Daily Allowance for calcium is twice that for phosphorous.
   B. Their absorption and utilization are enhanced by the presence of vitamin E.
   C. They are not found in soft tissues.
   D. They constitute an important buffer system in the regulation of body neutrality.

10. When a menu is being planned for a specific holiday, the one of the following which is LEAST appropriate is to

    A. ask for suitable menu possibilities from the staff
    B. choose only foods which are familiar to those who will be served
    C. test acceptability of possible holiday items by serving one or two items at earlier meals
    D. include traditional foods associated with the holiday, if available

11. When a No. 8 scoop is used to serve mashed potatoes, the portion served should be _____ cup.

    A. 2/5    B. 1/3    C. 1/2    D. 2/3

12. A six-ounce ladle is equal to APPROXIMATELY _____ cup(s).

    A. 1/2    B. 1    C. 3/4    D. 1 1/4

13. The MOST accurate measurement of food is by

    A. volume
    B. weight
    C. can size
    D. number of pieces per container

14. Deep fat frying is BEST accomplished at which one of the following temperatures?

    A. 300° F    B. 350° F    C. 400° F    D. 450° F

15. When you are roasting beef, the indication that a well-done and palatable product has been achieved is an interior temperature in the range of

    A. 110° to 130° F
    C. 151° to 170° F
    B. 131° to 150° F
    D. 171° to 190° F

16. Of the following methods of roasting beef, the one that causes the LEAST amount of shrinkage is cooking at

    A. high temperature during the first half of the cooking time and at low temperature during the other half
    B. high temperature during the entire cooking time

C. moderate temperature during the first half of the cooking time and at high temperature during the other half
D. low temperature during the entire cooking time

17. The method of meat preparation that calls for cutting the meat into small pieces, covering with hot liquid, and cooking at about 185° F is known as

   A. boiling    B. stewing    C. roasting    D. broiling

17._____

18. Of the following pressure ranges, the one in which three compartment steamers operate is the _____ lb. range.

   A. 1-5    B. 5-15    C. 15-30    D. 30-50

18._____

19. When vegetables are cooked for large numbers of people, the BEST results are obtained by *batch cooking*.
   This kind of cooking is done in order to

   A. have high-quality vegetables available during the entire serving period
   B. prepare more vegetables using less staff
   C. use less equipment
   D. prepare several batches of vegetables at the same time

19._____

20. The one of the following procedures that could cause food poisoning is

   A. allowing cooked poultry to stand for an hour, slicing it, and covering it with broth, and holding it at room temperature for several hours
   B. keeping food mixtures on cafeteria counters for one hour
   C. cooking left-over food mixtures quickly by frequent stirring and then refrigerating in shallow pans
   D. chilling all ingredients for salads for at least one hour before preparation

20._____

21. When large numbers of people are to be served in a cafeteria setting, an estimate should be made each day of the quantity of food to be prepared and cooked.
   This is BEST done by which one of the following ways?

   A. Having the cook make a list of the previous day's leftovers.
   B. Considering previous sales of the same menu combinations, as well as the weather and any special events.
   C. Cooking as much food as the staff and equipment allow so as not to be caught short.
   D. Using the capacity of the seating area as a base.

21._____

22. Which one of the following statements concerning frozen pre-cooked foods is NOT correct?

   A. Certain pre-cooked foods are excellent when freshly prepared, but deteriorate rapidly in an ordinary freezer.
   B. Some pre-cooked foods are so greatly changed by freezing and subsequent reheating that they become unpalatable.
   C. All food items which are carefully cooked, rapidly frozen, and then held at low temperature until used, are satisfactory products when served.
   D. Many foods may be frozen, stored in an appropriate type of freezer, and thawed without marked change in nutritional and esthetic value.

22._____

23. Of the following, the one which is NOT a method of controlling food costs in an institutional food service is

    A. avoiding the use of *leftover* foods since they are usually unpopular items
    B. maintaining an accurate food inventory
    C. knowing what yield can be obtained from various sizes, counts, and amounts of food
    D. ensuring the food-service employees use standardized recipes and portions

24. The direct labor cost involved in the preparation of meals includes wages paid to cooks, bakers, salad makers, counter workers, etc. and is MOST accurately determined by which one of the following methods?

    A. Making studies of the amount of time spent by employees in actual meal preparation tasks.
    B. Checking employees' time cards to determine total absence time.
    C. Dividing the number of meals served each week by the number of employees.
    D. Determining how much time is lost because of equipment breakdown and adding the value of this time to the cost of employees' wages.

25. Which one of the following would MOST likely enable the supervisor of a food service to attain better cost control over operations?

    A. *Increasing* the output of individual staff members.
    B. *Increasing* the size of the staff.
    C. *Reducing* the amount of time scheduled for food preparation tasks.
    D. *Reducing* the amount of time spent on training staff members.

## KEY (CORRECT ANSWERS)

| | | | |
|---|---|---|---|
| 1. | D | 11. | C |
| 2. | C | 12. | C |
| 3. | B | 13. | B |
| 4. | B | 14. | B |
| 5. | A | 15. | D |
| 6. | A | 16. | D |
| 7. | A | 17. | B |
| 8. | A | 18. | B |
| 9. | D | 19. | A |
| 10. | B | 20. | A |

21. B
22. C
23. A
24. A
25. A

# TEST 2

DIRECTIONS: Each question or incomplete statement is followed by several suggested answers or completions. Select the one that BEST answers the question or completes the statement. *PRINT THE LETTER OF THE CORRECT ANSWER IN THE SPACE AT THE RIGHT.*

1. Of the following, the FIRST step in the control of food costs in an institution should be to

    A. make sure the delivery of foods is in accordance with the order
    B. store foods under tight security as soon as they are received
    C. follow purchase specifications in obtaining food products
    D. get the correct amount of raw food to the cook

2. Of the following, the area in which recipe costing aids are of MOST value is

    A. making yield studies
    B. planning menus
    C. taking inventories
    D. determining the cost of wasted foods

3. Control records of both the physical and cost aspects of food storage are MOST useful as a basic guide in which one of the following areas?

    A. Receiving food deliveries
    B. Issuing food to the kitchen
    C. Ordering food
    D. Controlling food theft

4. The one of the following which indicates actual control over food costs in a food service is that

    A. recipe costing is done
    B. waste is eliminated
    C. yield studies are made
    D. food cost data are regularly analyzed

5. The one of the following which is the MAJOR purpose of a perpetual inventory in the food storage area of a kitchen or other dietary unit is to

    A. facilitate removal of shelf items that are needed for quick use
    B. reduce breakage and spoilage of liquified foods
    C. act as a control in the area of food purchasing
    D. facilitate the planning of balanced diets and menus

6. Walk-in storage refrigerators can be a very important aspect of a well-equipped kitchen in a food service.
   Of the following, the MOST desirable location for a walk-in refrigerator is near the

    A. receiving and preparation areas
    B. tray delivery area
    C. cafeteria
    D. dishwashing area

7. Food specifications are precise statements of quality and other commodity requirements. All food should be purchased according to specifications.
Of the following, the LEAST important aspect of a food specification is the

   A. quantity required in a case, pound, carton, etc.
   B. federal grade desired
   C. size of the container
   D. picture of the item

8. The aim in buying food is to obtain the best value for the money spent.
Of the following, the practice which is LEAST likely to accomplish that aim is

   A. buying the cheapest item
   B. purchasing by specification
   C. purchasing only the quantities required for the menus planned
   D. checking all purchases on delivery

9. When deciding whether to select a particular piece of equipment for a kitchen or other dietary area, the one of the following which would be LEAST important for you to take into consideration is

   A. whether there is space for it
   B. whether it is easily cleaned and maintained
   C. whether there is an employee currently on staff who knows how to operate it
   D. how well it has worked in other institutions

10. Of the following foods, the type that is MOST likely to cause staph food poisoning if improperly prepared or handled is _____ food.

    A. sugar-coated        B. dried
    C. pickled             D. cream-filled

11. Harmful bacteria are MOST often introduced into foods prepared in a food service operation by

    A. insects    B. rodents    C. employees    D. utensils

12. When planning menus for secondary school students, it is desirable for the manager to do all of the following EXCEPT to

    A. stay within the school's food budget
    B. include familiar ethnic foods
    C. include many food choices
    D. consider the size of the food service staff

13. Of the following, the manager's BEST evidence for a shortage claim on surplus food delivered to a school is

    A. her written report of the shortage claim
    B. the delivery receipt from the truck driver
    C. the container the food was delivered in
    D. an old container of the same item

14. The manager should prepare school lunch menus for a MINIMUM of _____ week(s) at a time.  14._____

    A. one   B. two   C. three   D. four

15. The manager must keep monthly inventories of all of the following EXCEPT  15._____

    A. paper goods
    B. food items
    C. serving utensils
    D. cleaning supplies

16. In the Type A lunch pattern for 10- to 12-year-old children, all of the following fulfill the *meat or meat alternate* requirement EXCEPT  16._____

    A. two ounces of cheese
    B. one-half cup of fresh carrots
    C. four tablespoons of peanut butter
    D. one-half cup of cooked dry peas

17. A manager is planning to use tuna fish salad to comply with the guideline for the *meat or meat alternate* requirement of the Type A lunch for secondary school students. How much tuna fish will she need in order to serve 400 secondary school students? _____ pounds.  17._____

    A. $37\frac{1}{2}$   B. 50   C. 75   D. 100

Questions 18-25.

DIRECTIONS: Answer Questions 18 through 25 SOLELY on the basis of information presented in the charts below.

### STUDENT SALES COUNTER SHEET
March 4, 2005

| Item | Price per Item | No. Items Offered for Sale | No. Items Unsold | Total Cash Received for Items Sold |
|---|---|---|---|---|
| Hot lunch | $2.25 | 250 | 75 | |
| Milk | $0.60 | 525 | | $285.00 |
| Soda | $0.75 | 300 | 163 | $102.75 |
| Ice Cream Bars | $0.45 | 181 | 59 | $54.90 |
| Buttered Roll | $0.15 | 200 | 150 | |
| Cooked Vegetable | $0.90 | 325 | 40 | $256.50 |
| Pudding | $0.45 | 565 | 30 | $240.75 |
| Potato Chips | $0.30 | 610 | 50 | $168.00 |

4 (#2)

## STUDENT SALES COUNTER SHEET
March 5, 2005

| Item | Price per Item | No. Items Offered for Sale | No. Items Unsold | Total Cash Received for Items Sold |
|---|---|---|---|---|
| Hot lunch | $2.25 | 300 | | $585.00 |
| Milk | $0.60 | 450 | | $255.00 |
| Soda | $0.75 | 275 | 207 | |
| Ice Cream Bars | $0.45 | 250 | 100 | |
| Buttered Roll | $0.15 | 175 | 25 | |
| Cooked Vegetable | $0.90 | 300 | 62 | $214.20 |
| Pudding | $0.45 | 490 | 47 | |
| Potato Chips | $0.30 | 595 | 45 | |

18. Hot lunches accounted for APPROXIMATELY what percentage of all cash received for March 4, 2005?   18.____

    A. 10%   B. 15%   C. 20%   D. 25%

19. Which one of the following items was sold LEAST on March 4, 2005 and March 5, 2005, combined?   19.____

    A. Soda   B. Ice cream bars
    C. Buttered roll   D. Cooked vegetable

20. The number of milk containers which were unsold on March 4, 2005 is   20.____

    A. 30   B. 50   C. 75   D. 95

21. How many fewer containers of pudding and soda were sold on March 5, 2005 than were sold on March 4, 2005?   21.____

    A. 19   B. 81   C. 105   D. 161

22. Which single item, besides hot lunches, accounted for the GREATEST number of items sold on March 4, 2005?   22.____

    A. Cooked vegetable   B. Pudding
    C. Ice cream bars   D. Soda

23. How many hot lunches were sold on March 4, 2005 and March 5, 2005, combined?   23.____

    A. 435   B. 550   C. 625   D. 665

24. Of the following, the item that was bought MOST by the students on both March 4, 2005 and March 5, 2005 is   24.____

    A. soda   B. buttered roll
    C. pudding   D. potato chips

25. The cumulative total of money received for all the soda, ice cream bars, buttered rolls, and pudding sold on March 4, 2005 is   25.____

    A. $165.15   B. $405.90   C. $858.90   D. $1252.65

## KEY (CORRECT ANSWERS)

1. C
2. B
3. C
4. B
5. C

6. A
7. D
8. A
9. C
10. D

11. C
12. C
13. C
14. D
15. C

16. B
17. C
18. D
19. C
20. B

21. D
22. B
23. A
24. D
25. B

# EXAMINATION SECTION
# TEST 1

DIRECTIONS: Each question or incomplete statement is followed by several suggested answers or completions. Select the one that BEST answers the question or completes the statement. *PRINT THE LETTER OF THE CORRECT ANSWER IN THE SPACE AT THE RIGHT.*

1. In food service operations, the supervisor usually can arrive at a decision concerning an operations problem by considering the following steps to a solution:
    I. Analysis of available information
    II. Definition of problem
    III. Development of alternate solutions
    IV. Selection of decision
    In which of the following options are the steps given in PROPER sequence?

    A. II, I, III, IV
    B. I, III, II, IV
    C. I, II, III, IV
    D. III, I, II, IV

    1.____

2. The one of the following which is MOST important for improvement of the productivity of food-service employees is the

    A. use of convenience foods
    B. posting of food preparation schedules for employees
    C. adoption and implementation of a program of task analysis and work measurement
    D. advance preparation of as much food as possible

    2.____

3. Assume that all of the following problems are occurring in a kitchen under your supervision: production is slow in terms of food preparation; housekeeping is lax; the quality of the food prepared is very poor; morale is low.
    Of these four problems, the one that is *most likely* the cause of all the others and should probably be attended to FIRST is

    A. slow production
    B. lax housekeeping
    C. poorly prepared food
    D. low morale

    3.____

4. A common problem in food-service supervision is that improper supervisory practices can lead to situations in which subordinates disobey direct orders given to them by their superior.
    Which of the following supervisors would be *most likely* to promote such a situation? A supervisor who

    A. does not delegate authority
    B. does not make a decision without consulting his or her entire staff
    C. is unwilling to punish any employee for an infraction of the rules
    D. rarely holds meetings with his or her staff

    4.____

5. While reviewing kitchen operations, you notice that a recently-hired employee is using too large a scoop for serving mashed potatoes. Since you personally instructed this individual in the proper utilization of serving utensils, you believe that this employee should be reprimanded.
    In this situation, the *most appropriate* of the following actions would be to

    5.____

11

A. call the employee aside, inform him of his mistake, and plan for additional instruction
B. inform the employee of his mistake in the presence of the other employees
C. remove the employee from his work station and assign him to some less desirable tasks
D. assign another employee to serve the mashed potatoes with the appropriate size scoop and have the recently-hired employee observe

6. Assume that you are approached individually by two employees who work together in food preparation. Each employee registers her complaint against working with the other. Which one of the following would be the MOST effective action to take in order to handle this problem?

    A. At the next regularly scheduled staff meeting, mention the importance of good working relationships.
    B. Ask your superior to make a judgment in this case, instead of deciding what to do yourself.
    C. Reassign one employee to a suitable job where she will not have to work with the other employee.
    D. Write a report to your superior detailing the problem and requesting transfers for both of the employees.

7. Suppose that, as a supervisor, you have an idea for changing the way a certain task is performed by your staff so that it will be less tedious and get done faster.
Of the following, the MOST advisable action for you to take regarding this idea is to

    A. issue a written memorandum, explaining the new method and giving reasons why it is to replace the old one
    B. discuss it with your staff to get their reactions and suggestions
    C. set up a training class in the new method for your staff
    D. try it out on an experimental basis on half the staff

8. In preparing work schedules for food-service employees, the one of the following considerations to which the supervisor should give LEAST priority is the

    A. work skills of the employees
    B. jobs to be done
    C. physical set-up of the work area and equipment available
    D. preferences of the employees

9. A new employee complains to you that she thinks the current method of serving meals is very ineffective. This employee strongly insists that another method is much better. However, the suggested method had been tried in the past with very unsatisfactory results. Of the following, the BEST way for you to handle the situation would be to

    A. assign the employee to a different work area to avoid conflict
    B. try out the suggested method for one or two days to demonstrate why it doesn't work
    C. briefly tell the employee that her suggested method will not work
    D. discuss with the employee the reasons why the present method has proven to be more successful than her suggested method

10. Assume that you find it necessary to discipline two subordinates, Mr. Tate and Mr. Sawyer, for coming to work late on several occasions. Their latenesses have had disruptive effects on the work schedule, and you have given both of them several verbal warnings. Mr. Tate has been in your work unit for many years, and his work has always been satisfactory. Mr. Sawyer is a probationary employee who has had some problems in learning your procedures. You decide to give Mr. Tate one more warning, in private, for his latenesses.
According to good supervisory practice, which one of the following disciplinary actions should you take with regard to Mr. Sawyer?

   A. Give him a reprimand in front of his co-workers to make a lasting impression.
   B. Recommend dismissal since he has not yet completed his probationary period.
   C. Give him one more warning, in private, for his latenesses.
   D. Recommend a short suspension or payroll deduction to impress on him the importance of coming to work on time.

10.____

11. Assume that you have delegated a very important work assignment to Johnson, one of your most experienced subordinates. Prior to completion of the assignment, your superior accidentally discovers that the assignment is being carried out incorrectly and tells you about it.
Which one of the following responses is *most appropriate* for you to give to your superior?

   A. "I take full responsibility, and I will see to it that the assignment is carried out correctly."
   B. "Johnson has been with us for many years now and should know better."
   C. "It really isn't Johnson's fault, rather it is the fault of the ancient equipment we have to do the job."
   D. "I think you should inform Johnson since he is the one at fault, not I."

11.____

12. Assume that you observe that one of your employees is talking excessively with other employees, quitting early and taking unusually long rest periods. Despite these abuses, she is one of your most productive employees, and her work is usually of the highest quality.
Of the following, the *most appropriate* action to take with regard to this employee is to

   A. ignore these infractions since she is one of your best workers
   B. ask your superior to reprimand her so that you can remain on the employee's good side
   C. reprimand her since not doing so would lower the morale of the other employees
   D. ask another of your subordinates to mention these infractions to the offending employee and suggest that she stop breaking rules

12.____

13. Assume that you have noticed that an employee whose attendance had been quite satisfactory is now showing marked evidence of a consistent pattern of absences.
Of the following, the BEST way to cope with this problem is to

   A. wait several weeks to see whether this pattern continues
   B. meet with the employee to try to find out the reasons for this change
   C. call a staff meeting and discuss the need for good attendance
   D. write a carefully worded warning to the employee

13.____

14. It is generally agreed that the successful supervisor must know how to wisely delegate work to her subordinates since she cannot do everything herself.
Which one of the following practices is *most likely* to result in INEFFECTIVE delegation by a supervisor?

   A. Establishment of broad controls to assure feedback about any deviations from plans
   B. Willingness to let subordinates use their own ideas about how to get the job done, where appropriate
   C. Constant observance of employees to see if they are making any mistakes
   D. Granting of enough authority to make possible the accomplishment of the delegated work

15. Suppose that, in accordance with grievance procedures, an employee brings a complaint to you, his immediate supervisor.
In dealing with his complaint, the one of the following which is MOST important for you to do is to

   A. talk to the employee's co-workers to learn whether the complaint is justified
   B. calm the employee by assuring him that you will look into the matter as soon as possible
   C. tell your immediate superior about the employee's complaint
   D. give the employee an opportunity to tell the full story

16. The successful application by a supervisor of work simplification techniques to food preparation and service work is *most likely* to result in which one of the following?

   A. Employees working harder than before
   B. Food products of higher nutritional value
   C. Better employee attendance
   D. Elimination of unnecessary parts of jobs

17. Holding staff meetings at regular Intervals is generally considered to be a good supervisory practice.
Which one of the following subjects is LEAST desirable for discussion at such a meeting?

   A. Revisions in agency personnel policies
   B. Violation of an agency rule by one of the employees present
   C. Problems of waste and breakage in the work area
   D. Complaints of employees about working conditions

18. Suppose that you are informed that your staff is soon to be reduced by one-third due to budget problems.
Which one of the following steps would be LEAST advisable in your effort to maintain a quality service with the smaller number of employees?

   A. Directing employees to speed up operations
   B. Giving employees training or retraining
   C. Rearranging the work area
   D. Revising work methods

19. Of the following, which action on the part of the supervisor is LEAST likely to contribute to upgrading the skills of her subordinates?  19._____

    A. Providing appropriate training to subordinates
    B. Making periodic evaluations of subordinates and discussing the evaluations with the subordinates
    C. Consistently assigning subordinates to those tasks with which they are familiar
    D. Giving increased responsibility to appropriate subordinates

20. Suppose that a new employee on your staff has difficulty in performing his assigned tasks, after having been given training.  20._____
    Of the following courses of action, the one which would be BEST for you, his supervisor, to take FIRST is to

    A. change his work assignment
    B. give him a poor evaluation since he is obviously unable to do the work
    C. give him the training again
    D. have him work with an employee who is more experienced in the tasks for a short while

21. To insure the safety of employees who must retrieve items from a food storeroom, the supervisor should direct that  21._____

    A. bulky items be put on the floor near the storeroom door
    B. newly-received items be put on the shelves in front of previously-received items
    C. ladders or step-stools be used to reach upper shelves
    D. frequently-requisitioned items be piled up just outside the entrance to the storeroom

22. Suppose that a cook receives a minor burn, which causes a blister on his hand, while handling a hot pan of food. After seeing that the employee gets proper treatment for the burn, the MOST advisable of the following actions for the supervisor to take is to  22._____

    A. send the employee home
    B. tell the employee to return to his work station
    C. help the employee to finish the day's food preparation
    D. temporarily assign the employee to a task other than handling food

23. Of the following, the FIRST step which should be taken by you, the supervisor, in the orientation of a new food-service employee is to  23._____

    A. include the new employee in the next regularly-scheduled staff conference
    B. discuss with the new employee the many problems which the kitchen staff faces daily
    C. give the new employee a task to see how well he can perform
    D. have a conference with the new employee and discuss what his duties will be

24. Assume that, as part of a step-by-step training process, the supervisor explained and demonstrated a food preparation task to a new employee. As a last step, the supervisor told the employee to perform the task himself.  24._____
    The training given by this supervisor was

A. *good;* by putting the employee on his own, the supervisor indicated confidence in the employee
B. *poor;* he didn't ask whether the employee understood how to perform the task
C. *good;* he employed the technique of demonstration
D. *poor;* more than one instructor is required to make this method of training effective

25. Of the following, the BEST way to follow-up immediately after giving a new employee training in food preparation tasks is to

   A. have the new employee observe more experienced employees performing their tasks
   B. give the new employee an overall view of all the food service operations
   C. allow the new employee to perform the tasks herself under careful supervision
   D. have the new employee write a report on what she has learned

26. If one of your kitchen staff performs a particularly important task incorrectly, the one of the following times which is BEST for teaching her the proper procedure so that she will remember it is

   A. later on in the day after she has had time to think about the task
   B. immediately so that she can correct her error
   C. after the workday ends so you may speak to her with less distraction
   D. during the next regularly-scheduled staff training session

27. Assume that you are approached by a cook who is upset and who wants to give you her explanation as to why the day's food preparation went wrong.
In order to be an understanding listener, you should do ALL of the following EXCEPT

   A. carefully question the worker
   B. make a value judgment so you can take a definite position on the matter
   C. try to find out the meaning of the emotions behind the cook's statements
   D. restate the cook's position to assure that you comprehend what she is telling you

28. A troubled subordinate privately approaches his supervisor in order to talk about a problem on the job.
In this situation, the one of the following actions that is NOT desirable on the part of the supervisor is to

   A. ask the subordinate pertinent questions to help develop points further
   B. close his office door during the talk to block noisy distractions
   C. allow sufficient time to complete the discussion with the subordinate
   D. take over the conversation so the employee won't be embarrassed

29. Suppose that one of your goals as a supervisor is to foster good working relationships between yourself and your employees, without undermining your supervisory effectiveness by being too friendly.
Of the following, the BEST way to achieve this goal when dealing with employees' work problems is to

   A. discourage individual personal conferences by using regularly scheduled staff meetings to discuss work problems
   B. try to resolve work problems within a relatively short period of time

C. insist that employees put all work problems into writing before seeing you
D. maintain an open-door policy, allowing employees complete freedom of access to you without making appointments to discuss work problems

30. Of the following duties, the one that may be performed by a designated employee instead of the manager is  30.____

    A. preparing work schedules for each job in the kitchen
    B. placing all orders for food
    C. checking, counting, and weighing supplies received
    D. tasting all cooked foods, salads, sandwich and dessert mixtures

## KEY (CORRECT ANSWERS)

| | | |
|---|---|---|
| 1. A | 11. A | 21. C |
| 2. C | 12. C | 22. D |
| 3. D | 13. B | 23. D |
| 4. C | 14. C | 24. B |
| 5. A | 15. D | 25. C |
| 6. C | 16. D | 26. B |
| 7. B | 17. B | 27. B |
| 8. D | 18. A | 28. D |
| 9. D | 19. C | 29. B |
| 10. C | 20. D | 30. C |

# EXAMINATION SECTION
# TEST 1

DIRECTIONS: Each question or incomplete statement is followed by several suggested answers or completions. Select the one that BEST answers the question or completes the statement. *PRINT THE LETTER OF THE CORRECT ANSWER IN THE SPACE AT THE RIGHT.*

1. Of the following, the requisition which is CORRECT for the number of servings indicated is

    A. 300 lbs. eviscerated frozen turkey for 480 servings
    B. 190 lbs. cured ham, bone in, for ham steaks for 600 servilngs
    C. 100 lbs. whole beef liver for 520 servings
    D. 380 lbs. veal leg, bone in, for roast veal for 500 servings

    1.____

2. Of the following, the LEAST effective way of effecting portion control is by means of

    A. instruction of personnel responsible for serving food
    B. purchase of pre-portioned foods
    C. use of standardized serving utensils
    D. preparation and use of standardized recipes

    2.____

3. The MOST important reason for using a manual in a dietary department is that it serves as a

    A. means of preventing duplication of work
    B. tool for achieving orderly operations
    C. system for controlling food waste
    D. system for controlling food costs

    3.____

4. Of the following, the MOST important reason for using standardized recipes is that they provide

    A. uniformity of quality and quantity of the product
    B. greater control of raw food costs
    C. saving of labor hours resulting in lower cost
    D. guidance in pre-planning of menus

    4.____

5. From the standpoint of the dietitian, the CHIEF advantage of centralized as compared to decentralized food service is that

    A. space needed for floor pantries in a decentralized service can be used instead for other purposes
    B. better controls can be exercised by the dietitian
    C. less service is required from the nursing department
    D. it eliminates complaints that pantry noises on the floor disturb the patients

    5.____

6. Assume that the dishwashing load is unusually heavy for the facilities provided. Of the following, the MOST expedient method for reducing the load would be to

    A. stagger the meal hours
    B. use paper cups for beverages

    6.____

2 (#1)

C. increase the number of employees handling the operation
D. decrease the timing on the machine wash and rinse operations

7. The amount of freezer space necessary in a kitchen will depend MAINLY upon the    7.____

   A. frequency of delivery service
   B. amount of money that can be tied up in stored items
   C. number of frozen foods used on the menu
   D. savings effected in purchasing in bulk at advantageous times

8. Before recommending a time-saving device, the MOST important factor to be considered is    8.____

   A. whether it will be used frequently
   B. the amount of maintenance which will be required
   C. the number of productive labor hours which will be saved
   D. the space it will require

9. Before planning a kitchen layout, it is MOST important to know    9.____

   A. how much money will be available
   B. the relation of the kitchen to other areas
   C. the numbers and availability of personnel
   D. what types of menus and service will be used

10. Kitchen equipment should be placed PRIMARILY to    10.____

    A. provide neat, uncluttered appearance
    B. avoid cross traffic
    C. permit easy access to the main delivery area
    D. establish a separate work area for each cook

11. The MAIN advantage of using standardized pans is that    11.____

    A. the same pan can be used for cooking, serving, and storing
    B. fewer pans are required
    C. they stack better and require less storage space
    D. less time is used to select the right pan for the job

12. Specific cleaning agents and detergents have been recommended for use on various surface materials in order to do a thorough job of cleaning and to maintain the attractive appearance of the material.    12.____
    Of the following, the one which you would recommend for the purpose indicated is

    A. tri-sodium phosphate for cleaning aluminum pots and pans
    B. a scouring cleanser with a high percent of abrasive material for cleaning stainless steel tables and trucks
    C. a lye base liquid soap for use in automatic dishwashing machines
    D. a non-oil base detergent for floors covered with light-colored rubber tile

13. Scraping and prerinsing of dishes before running them through the dishwashing machine is necessary to    13.____

A. shorten the time of the washing process
B. reduce the amount of detergent needed
C. prevent blocking of the nozzles in the rinse arm of the machine
D. remove food particles which harden at the wash temperature

14. When purchasing food, the one of the following which should be the deciding factor for determining what is the MOST economical buy is the

    A. unit price as purchased
    B. cost of edible portion
    C. cost of product as served
    D. preparation costs

15. When ordering perishable foods, the specification should designate the condition of the foods as of the time of

    A. delivery    B. shipment    C. packaging    D. bidding

16. Of the following forms in which meat can be purchased, the form which makes possible MOST accurate portion control is

    A. quarters              B. prefabricated
    C. carcass               D. wholesale cuts

17. Fresh fruits are generally at their best during certain periods.
    Of the following, the statement which is LEAST accurate is that

    A. cherries are best in June and July
    B. cranberries are best from April to September
    C. grapefruit is best from November to February
    D. California grapes are best from November to February

18. When labor is the MOST important consideration, it is BEST to purchase potatoes

    A. whole, unpeeled          B. whole, peeled
    C. instant, powdered        D. canned

19. When purchasing grapefruit for an institution, it is BEST to purchase by the

    A. pound    B. dozen    C. bushel    D. crate count

20. Of the following, the specification which is LEAST desirable when purchasing fresh vegetables is

    A. cauliflower, leaves trimmed to within 1" to 2" from head
    B. beets, stems completely removed
    C. carrots, topped, tops cut back to less than 1"
    D. celery, stalk length 16" and well trimmed

21. When accepting a delivery of a large order of frozen foods, it is MOST important to

    A. be sure that the grade which was ordered is received
    B. see that the labels are intact
    C. check for evidence of defrosting
    D. weigh the merchandise to be sure of correct weight

22. For proper storage of dry and canned food supplies, it is NOT advisable to    22._____

   A. place all shelving and stacks close against the wall to prevent falling
   B. stack like items together to facilitate issuing and taking of inventories
   C. store canned goods on shelves or on platforms 4 to 6" off the floor
   D. stack the most recent receipts in back or on the bottom to make the *first in, first out* rule easy to follow

23. If a high bacteria count on the dishes is found in one of the serving units, it is LEAST    23._____
    important to

   A. check the wash and rinse temperature of the dishwashing machine
   B. check the technique for scraping, prerinsing, washing, and rinsing dishes
   C. inspect the serving unit, including all equipment, for cleanliness
   D. arrange for a physical examination of every employee in the department

24. Rodent control is of prime importance in maintaining sanitary conditions.    24._____
    The MOST effective way to eliminate rodents is by

   A. providing regular visits of licensed exterminators
   B. use of traps baited with food
   C. cautious use of rat poisons
   D. elimination of harborages

25. The recommended daily dietary allowance of protein for an aged man is MOST NEARLY    25._____
    _____ gm. per kg. body weight.

   A. .5     B. 1     C. 1.5     D. 2

## KEY (CORRECT ANSWERS)

| | | | |
|---|---|---|---|
| 1. A | | 11. A | |
| 2. A | | 12. D | |
| 3. B | | 13. D | |
| 4. A | | 14. C | |
| 5. B | | 15. A | |
| 6. B | | 16. B | |
| 7. A | | 17. B | |
| 8. C | | 18. C | |
| 9. D | | 19. D | |
| 10. B | | 20. B | |

21. C
22. A
23. D
24. D
25. B

# TEST 2

DIRECTIONS: Each question or incomplete statement is followed by several suggested answers or completions. Select the one that BEST answers the question or completes the statement. *PRINT THE LETTER OF THE CORRECT ANSWER IN THE SPACE AT THE RIGHT.*

1. The GREATEST amount of protein per unit of body weight is needed during   1._____

    A. childhood    B. infancy    C. adolescence    D. pregnancy

2. The thiamine needs of the individual are dependent upon the   2._____

    A. total caloric intake    B. body weight
    C. body height             D. age

3. Of the following foods, the BEST source of riboflavin is   3._____

    A. lean meat    B. egg    C. milk    D. orange

4. Of the following groups of foods, the one which contains the LARGEST number of alkaline-ash foods is   4._____

    A. milk, sugar, and starch
    B. milk, meat, and potatoes
    C. all fruits and vegetables
    D. most fruits, most vegetables, and milk

5. Of the following nutrients, the one which may reduce the amount of radioactive strontium 90 which may be deposited in the body is   5._____

    A. vitamin D       B. calcium
    C. oleic acid      D. ascorbic acid

6. If taken in massive doses over a period of time, the vitamin which may cause toxic effects is   6._____

    A. ascorbic acid       B. pantothenic acid
    C. vitamin $B_{12}$    D. vitamin A

7. The vitamin which contains cobalt is   7._____

    A. vitamin $B_{12}$    B. folic acid
    C. ascorbic acid       D. riboflavin

8. The term *niacin equivalents* refers to   8._____

    A. foods which have an equivalent niacin content
    B. the increase necessary when metabolism is accelerated
    C. the quantitative tryptophan-niacin relationship
    D. the minimum amount of niacin which will protect against symptoms of pellagra

9. The blood cholesterol level is MOST affected by   9._____

    A. body cholesterol synthesis      B. ingestion of egg yolks
    C. total dietary cholesterol intake   D. total fat intake

10. The calcium is unavailable because it forms an insoluble salt in combination with oxalic acid in

   A. collards     B. carrots     C. beets     D. spinach

11. Following convalescence from gastric surgery, a relatively high proportion of patients experience distressing symptoms after eating.
   The diet prescription for this condition is USUALLY

   A. high protein, high fat, low carbohydrate
   B. high protein, low fat, low carbohydrate
   C. high protein, high carbohydrate, low fat
   D. low protein, low fat, high carbohydrate

12. An increase of high residue foods in the diet is indicated in cases of

   A. spastic constipation
   B. ulcerative colitis
   C. atonic constipation
   D. diverticulitis

13. The dietary treatment for diseases of the liver consists of

   A. high protein, high carbohydrate, and moderate fat intake
   B. moderate protein, low carbohydrate, and low fat intake
   C. high protein, moderate carbohydrate, and moderate fat intake
   D. moderate protein, high carbohydrate, and low fat intake

14. The diet USUALLY prescribed for persons with hyperchlorhydria is _____ diet.

   A. 100 mg. sodium
   B. low residue
   C. low phosphorus
   D. low purine

15. In the treatment of phenylketonuria, the diet MUST be modified so that

   A. all protein is eliminated from the diet
   B. phenylalanine is completely eliminated from the diet until the child is 5 years old
   C. the serum level of phenylalanine is maintained within normal limits
   D. milk and milk products are the only foods eliminated from the diet

16. When signs of impending hepatic coma appear in a patient with advanced cirrhosis, the diet MOST likely to be ordered is

   A. low protein
   B. low carbohydrate
   C. low caloric
   D. fat free

17. The one of the following menus which would be BEST to serve to an ulcer patient who follows kosher food laws is

   A. cream of pea soup, cream cheese sandwich, asparagus tips, custard, milk
   B. cream of pea soup, chicken, mashed potatoes, diced carrots, canned pears, milk
   C. tomato juice, beef pattie, baked potato with butter, peas, junket, milk
   D. apple juice, creamed diced shrimp on rice, peas, canned peaches, milk

18. In the treatment of gout, the one of the following which MUST often be restricted because it may inhibit the excretion of uric acid is

    A. carbohydrate   B. fats
    C. fluids         D. calcium

19. Of the following groups of foods, the one which may be indicated in a gluten-free diet is

    A. rye, barley, and macaroni
    B. crackers, spaghetti, and rice
    C. cream of wheat, cornstarch, and oats
    D. corn, potato, and rice

20. The one of the following which would NOT alleviate the symptoms of the dumping syndrome is

    A. small frequent feedings instead of large meals
    B. dry meals with fluids taken only between meals
    C. emphasis on concentrated forms of carbohydrates
    D. avoidance of chilled foods

21. The one of the following symptoms which is MOST indicative of riboflavin deficiency is

    A. poor wound healing
    B. fissures at the corners of the mouth
    C. bone deformities
    D. simple goiter

22. A preschool child who is allowed to drink as much as 2 quarts of milk daily to the exclusion of adequate amounts of solid foods is MOST likely to be deficient in

    A. protein    B. riboflavin    C. iron    D. vitamin A

23. The ketosis which occurs in uncontrolled diabetes is caused by the excessive oxidation of

    A. B-complex vitamins   B. fats
    C. carbohydrates        D. ascorbic acid

24. *Hidden hunger* may be the result of a diet lacking in sufficient amounts of

    A. foods high in cellulose   B. high calorie foods
    C. protein foods             D. protective foods

25. A possible result of protein deficiency is

    A. edema   B. heart disease
    C. gout    D. sprue

## KEY (CORRECT ANSWERS)

1. B
2. A
3. C
4. D
5. B

6. D
7. A
8. C
9. A
10. D

11. A
12. C
13. A
14. B
15. C

16. A
17. A
18. B
19. D
20. C

21. B
22. C
23. B
24. D
25. A

# TEST 3

DIRECTIONS: Each question or incomplete statement is followed by several suggested answers or completions. Select the one that BEST answers the question or completes the statement. *PRINT THE LETTER OF THE CORRECT ANSWER IN THE SPACE AT THE RIGHT.*

1. A negative nitrogen balance occurs when

    A. more nitrogen is being ingested than is excreted in the urine
    B. new tissue is being built in periods of rapid growth
    C. dietary protein intake is adequate for tissue synthesis
    D. the body's energy needs must be met from the body's stores of fat and the reserves of protein

    1._____

2. When planning a diet for an overweight adolescent girl, it is MOST important to consider that

    A. the chief problem is controlling the intake of candy and rich desserts
    B. overweight often disappears by the end of the adolescent period
    C. most problems of overweight are glandular in origin
    D. emotional and social problems are often related to the obesity

    2._____

3. If a patient with a long-term illness has anorexia, it is MOST important that

    A. he lie down for a half hour before each meal
    B. he be served his favorite foods first
    C. his nutritional requirements be met in spite of his lack of appetite
    D. he be allowed an alcoholic beverage as an appetite stimulant

    3._____

4. Assume that the bakers have been scheduled to be off duty on Saturday and Sunday. Under these circumstances, the MOST suitable one of the following combinations of desserts for Sunday is

    A. brownie a la mode for dinner; cheesecake (frozen) for supper
    B. apple pie a la mode for dinner; baked bread pudding for supper
    C. butterscotch pie for dinner; canned fruit cocktail with cookies for supper
    D. cherry jello with sliced bananas for dinner; Napoleons for supper

    4._____

5. To increase consumer satisfaction, it is recommended that whenever possible a choice of menu items be offered.
   Of the following, the choice of menu items which is LEAST appropriate for use in a hospital cafeteria is

    A. stewed prunes or fresh frozen orange juice
    B. half grapefruit or canned applesauce
    C. sliced bananas or baked applies
    D. pineapple juice or grapefruit sections

    5._____

27

6. When preparing the menu, it is important to consider ease in serving, overall economy, and utilization of manpower and supplies.
   Of the following menu items, the combination which is LEAST appropriate for a hospital menu is

   A. sliced tomato salad or head lettuce salad
   B. carrot and raisin salad or Waldorf salad
   C. coleslaw or celery and carrot sticks
   D. marinated sliced cucumbers or tossed salad greens

6.\_\_\_\_

7. Of the following, the one which BEST illustrates the principles of good menu planning is

   A. beef stew, creamed diced potatoes, mixed vegetable salad, bread, butter, chilled fruit cup, coffee, tea or milk
   B. baked stuffed pork chop, mashed potatoes, buttered broccoli, spiced applesauce, bread, butter, raspberry sherbet with vanilla cookies, coffee, tea or milk
   C. French fried shrimp, baked potato, fried eggplant, lettuce salad with Thousand Islands dressing, bread, butter, sugared doughnuts, coffee, tea or milk
   D. cream of celery soup, baked filet of sole, steamed diced potatoes, buttered cauliflower, bread, butter, lemon sherbet, coffee, tea or milk

7.\_\_\_\_

8. Assume that a disaster has occurred and you have no gas or electricity in your hospital but you have steam and hot water. The feeding census has doubled to 3000.
   The BEST of the following menus to serve under these circumstances is:

   A. steamed frankfurters, Creole lima beans, pickle slices, bread or rolls, butter, mustard, sliced pineapple, boxed cookies, coffee and milk
   B. cold cuts, potato salad, sliced tomatoes, bread, butter, mustard, fresh apples, coffee, milk
   C. tomato juice, hamburgers on a bun, sliced onion, coleslaw, potato chips, canned applesauce, coffee, milk
   D. egg salad on lettuce, baked potato, bread, butter, hot cocoa, canned fruit cocktail

8.\_\_\_\_

9. The timing of the cooking of fresh and frozen vegetables must be carefully planned into each day's operation if the final product is to be of top quality when it is served. When cooking vegetables in a steam kettle, the vegetables are added after the water comes to a boil and timing begins when the water reboils.
   Of the following, the one which would NOT result in a top quality product is cooking of twenty pounds of

   A. fresh broccoli for 15 to 20 minutes
   B. frozen peas for 25 to 30 minutes
   C. fresh asparagus for 5 to 10 minutes
   D. frozen chopped spinach for 10 to 15 minutes

9.\_\_\_\_

10. Advance preparation enables the dietary department to serve a variety of menu items not otherwise possible.
    The one of the following items which may be prepared 12 to 24 hours in advance without loss in quality is

    A. Brown Betty               B. stuffed pork chops
    C. potato salad              D. spiced pears

10.\_\_\_\_

11. When the butcher is instructed to process meat for beef stew, he should be instructed to use beef _____ and beef _____.

    A. chuck; neck
    B. loin; chuck
    C. round; ribs
    D. neck; loin

12. Of the following, the food items which are NOT interchangeable in recipes are

    A. chocolate with cocoa and fat
    B. fresh whole milk with non-fat dry milk solids and fat plus water
    C. baking powder with buttermilk and soda
    D. hard flour with soft flour and cornstarch

13. To produce the BEST medium white sauce, you should add for each cup of milk _____ of flour.

    A. 1 teaspoon
    B. 2 tablespoons
    C. 1/4 cup
    D. 8 tablespoons

14. The quality of food when served is greatly affected by the timing of preparation and cooking.
    The one of the following which is MOST likely to be of acceptable quality when served is

    A. corn on the cob husked in the morning, refrigerated in plastic bags until 3:30, and cooked for 25 minutes at 4 P.M. for evening meal hour 4:30 to 6 P.M.
    B. hamburgers made from beef freshly ground at 7 A.M., seasoned, shaped and panned at 9 A.M., cooked in oven at 10:30 A.M., and distributed to all dining rooms at 11:30 for noon service until 1 P.M.
    C. baked potatoes, sorted and washed the day before, panned at 7 A.M., placed in hot oven to bake at 20 minute intervals starting at 10:30 A.M., removed at same intervals starting at 11:15 A.M., pierced and sent to dining rooms for service starting at 11:30 A.M.
    D. jelly omelet made by skillet method by cracking eggs early in morning, frying omelets at 10:30 A.M., spreading and folding jelly into them, cutting into standard portions, and placing them in a warm oven to hold for serving at 11:30 to 1 P.M.

15. Of the following, the LEAST important consideration in planning menus is the

    A. facilities and equipment available for food preparation
    B. ethnic and cultural food habits of patients
    C. per capita budgetary allowance
    D. method of food service to be used

16. In planning alternate choices of food items on a selective menu, it is MOST important to list alternatives which are of approximately the same

    A. cost per portion
    B. food grouping
    C. degree of acceptability
    D. color and texture

17. Many hospitals favor the use of cycle menus to improve their food service. However, cycle menus should NOT be used to

    A. simplify menu writing
    B. promote standardization of recipes and food production procedures

C. provide a fixed, unalterable menu pattern
D. help maintain better cost control

18. The one of the following which is LEAST useful in computing raw food costs for a given period is the

    A. inventory records of foods received and issued
    B. unit and total costs of foods used
    C. records of overhead and salaries
    D. record of meals served

19. The one of the following which has LEAST value in pre-costing a menu before it is served is the

    A. desired portion size of each item
    B. cost of the ingredients
    C. cost of labor
    D. estimated number of portions required

20. When planning menus, one should try to include items which are generally acceptable to as many individuals as possible to reduce leftovers.
    Of the following, the food you should plan to use LEAST often in order to avoid excessive leftovers is

    A. chicken a la king          B. roast beef
    C. lettuce and tomato salad   D. chocolate layer cake

21. To maintain good standards of nutrition, the LARGEST percentage of the food dollar should be spent for

    A. cereal products    B. fruits and vegetables
    C. dairy products     D. meats

22. When giving diet instruction to a patient, the FIRST thing a dietitian should do is to

    A. explain the essentials of an adequate diet
    B. determine the amount of money available for food
    C. determine present and previous patterns of eating
    D. explain that a change in food habits will make the patient healthier

23. Assume that an older person asks for advice on how he can achieve greater enjoyment of meals and less distress after eating.
    Of the following, the suggestion you should NOT make is that he eat

    A. a good breakfast to start the day
    B. four or five light meals instead of three heavier meals
    C. mostly cereal products since these are easiest to prepare and masticate
    D. the heaviest meal at noon rather than at night if sleeping is difficult

24. Of the following, the MOST desirable dinner menu for a geriatric patient who is on a regular diet is

    A. grilled frankfurters, baked beans, cole slaw, baked apple
    B. pot roast, noodles, carrot timbale, applesauce

C. fried chicken, mashed potatoes, rutabagas, cheese strudel
D. broiled fish, French fried potatoes, broccoli, cherry pie

25. Of the following menus, the one which is LEAST acceptable from the point of view of good menu planning for a patient on a regular diet is   25.____

    A. roast lamb, mashed potatoes, buttered carrot rings, applesauce, bread and butter, cottage pudding with custard sauce, coffee, tea or milk
    B. simmered corned beef, parsley buttered potatoes, steamed cabbage wedge, horseradish and beet relish, bread and butter, fresh fruit cup, coffee, tea, milk
    C. Salisbury steak with mushroom gravy, French fried potatoes, sliced tomato salad on chicory, French dressing, vanilla ice cream, oatmeal cookie, coffee, tea, milk
    D. baked cured ham with mustard sauce, scalloped sweet potatoes with apples, cole slaw, bread and butter, Boston cream pie, coffee, tea, milk

# KEY (CORRECT ANSWERS)

| | | | |
|---|---|---|---|
| 1. | D | 11. | A |
| 2. | D | 12. | D |
| 3. | C | 13. | B |
| 4. | A | 14. | C |
| 5. | C | 15. | D |
| 6. | B | 16. | B |
| 7. | B | 17. | C |
| 8. | A | 18. | C |
| 9. | B | 19. | D |
| 10. | D | 20. | A |

| | |
|---|---|
| 21. | D |
| 22. | C |
| 23. | C |
| 24. | B |
| 25. | A |

# EXAMINATION SECTION
## TEST 1

DIRECTIONS: Each question or incomplete statement is followed by several suggested answers or completions. Select the one that BEST answers the question or completes the statement. *PRINT THE LETTER OF THE CORRECT ANSWER IN THE SPACE AT THE RIGHT.*

1. The one of the following groups of garnishes or accompaniments which is MOST appropriate for the entree designated is   1.____

   A. boiled beef; horseradish sour cream sauce, mixed pickles, beet and onion relish, lemon wedge
   B. roast veal; cranberry sauce, fried apple ring, parsley, French fried onion ring
   C. broiled fish; lemon wedge, tartar sauce, chopped parsley, lemon butter
   D. hamburger; sliced onion, catsup, French fried onion rings, Hollandaise sauce

2. Assume that the following menu has been submitted: chicken fricasee, mashed potatoes, cauliflower, bread and butter, applesauce, coffee, tea, milk.   2.____
   The CHIEF defect of this menu is that it is

   A. inadequate in protein content
   B. lacking in color and texture contrast
   C. improperly balanced as to nutrient content
   D. too high in calories

3. Assume that the following menu has been submitted for lunch: baked ham, pan browned parsnips, baked sweet potato, cornbread and butter, Apple Brown Betty with whipped topping.   3.____
   This menu is NOT well-planned primarily because

   A. there are too many calories
   B. there are no vitamin C foods
   C. there is not enough variety in texture of the foods
   D. the workload is not well distributed for the kitchen's cooking equipment

4. If a patient on a diabetic diet dislikes milk, he may exchange the milk with one   4.____

   A. bread exchange, one meat exchange, and one fat exchange
   B. fruit exchange
   C. bread exchange, one beverage, and one fat exchange
   D. meat exchange and one fruit exchange

5. The one of the following foods which can be used by a diabetic patient as a substitute in a meat exchange is   5.____

   A. ice cream
   B. cheddar cheese
   C. lima beans
   D. blackeye peas

6. Of the following foods, the one which should NOT be included in a clear liquid diet is   6.____

   A. milk
   B. fat-free broth
   C. fruit or vegetable juice
   D. carbonated beverages

7. The one of the following which is permitted on a 500 mg. sodium diet is

   A. cornflakes
   B. rice krispies
   C. puffed wheat
   D. wheat flakes

8. The one of the following statements which is INCORRECT is that riboflavin

   A. helps the cells utilize oxygen
   B. helps keep vision clear
   C. prevents cracking of mouth corners
   D. helps the body absorb calcium

9. The one of the following which is NOT concerned with the digestion of fat is

   A. cholecystokinin
   B. lipase
   C. bile
   D. ptyalin

10. The diet which should be given to a patient who has chronic kidney disease with nitrogen retention is

    A. high protein, low carbohydrate
    B. low protein
    C. low calcium, low phosphorus
    D. low purine

11. The diet MOST likely to be ordered for the pernicious vomiting of pregnancy is

    A. high carbohydrate, low fat
    B. high carbohydrate, high fat, high protein
    C. low carbohydrate, low fat, high protein
    D. high protein, low sodium

12. In the treatment of hemorrhagic and nutritional anemias, the MOST important nutrients to stress are iron and

    A. protein     B. vitamin A     C. iodine     D. vitamin E

13. The USUAL diet for a patient with acute gallbladder is a _____ diet.

    A. low fat
    B. 1000 mg. sodium
    C. high protein
    D. low cholesterol

14. Assume that a leukemia patient has difficulty swallowing the foods prescribed for her. In order to provide a diet which is nutritionally adequate, it is LEAST advisable to recommend

    A. a liquid diet emphasizing high caloric liquids and protein supplements
    B. nasal tube feeding in order to meet all nutritional requirements and to avoid the problem of swallowing
    C. a diet on which the meat is minced and all fruits and vegetables are pureed
    D. a diet similar to the one prescribed for her except that each item is pureed

15. The diet MOST likely to be prescribed for a patient who has renal stones is a(n) _____ diet.

    A. elimination
    B. low oxalate
    C. low cholesterol
    D. high carbohydrate, low protein, low fat

16. A rice diet is USUALLY prescribed for patients who

    A. have high blood pressure
    B. have a food allergy
    C. are recovering from a gallbladder operation
    D. require a high caloric intake

17. Patients suffering severe burns are MOST likely to have

    A. loss of serum protein
    B. steatorrhea
    C. polyneuritis
    D. stomatitis

18. Of the following statements concerning phenylketonuria, the one that is NOT correct is that it

    A. is caused by an enzyme deficiency
    B. leads to mental retardation
    C. is treated by the restriction of carbohydrates
    D. must be detected in the first few months of life in order to be treated

19. During all periods of growth, vitamin D is essential for efficient absorption and utilization of

    A. calcium and potassium
    B. potassium and iron
    C. magnesium and calcium
    D. phosphorus and calcium

20. In the treatment of urinary calculi, the one of the following which will assist in maintaining an acid urine is

    A. cranberry juice
    B. peas
    C. cabbage
    D. corn oil

21. Of the following, the food containing the HIGHEST amount of thiamine per 100 gram portion is

    A. fresh green peas
    B. fresh pork
    C. fresh spinach
    D. ground beef

22. The one of the following foods which is the POOREST source of niacin per 100 gram portion is

    A. lean meats
    B. peanuts
    C. whole grain cereals
    D. green leafy vegetables

23. Of the following lists of foods, the one which will contribute MOST to the ascorbic acid content of a diet is

    A. potatoes, green peppers, raw cabbage
    B. enriched bread, pork, turnips
    C. whole wheat bread, potatoes, prunes
    D. apples, dates, plums

24. Of the following foods, the content of unsaturated fatty acids is GREATEST in

    A. butter
    B. corn oil
    C. beef suet
    D. lard

25. Of the following, the one with the LOWEST vitamin C content per 4 oz. portion is _____ juice.   25.\_\_\_\_

   A. orange
   B. lemon
   C. tomato
   D. grapefruit

---

# KEY (CORRECT ANSWERS)

1. C
2. B
3. D
4. A
5. B

6. A
7. C
8. D
9. D
10. B

11. A
12. A
13. A
14. C
15. B

16. A
17. A
18. C
19. D
20. A

21. B
22. D
23. A
24. B
25. C

---

# TEST 2

DIRECTIONS: Each question or incomplete statement is followed by several suggested answers or completions. Select the one that BEST answers the question or completes the statement. *PRINT THE LETTER OF THE CORRECT ANSWER IN THE SPACE AT THE RIGHT.*

1. When roasting meat, the GREATEST yield of finished product may be expected when      1.____

    A. it is quickly seared on both sides at the beginning
    B. a high temperature is used throughout the roasting period
    C. a small quantity of water is added during roasting
    D. a low temperature is used throughout the roasting process

2. Of the following, the meat which is LEAST suitable for roasting is      2.____

    A. loin of pork
    B. corned brisket
    C. rump of veal
    D. leg of lamb

3. The loss of weight which results from braising boneless bottom round of beef, when proper techniques are used, is      3.____

    A. negligible
    B. about 10%
    C. about 25%
    D. over 50%

4. Of the following, the one which gives the MOST appropriate cooking temperature for the food indicated is      4.____

    A. beef loaf - 450° F
    B. baked potatoes - 250° F
    C. caramel custard - 325° F
    D. gingerbread - 475° F

5. In teaching a *cook trainee* how to deep fat fry various items of food, one should NOT instruct him to      5.____

    A. lower the food into the fat quickly
    B. make uniform portions of food for frying in the same load
    C. fill frying baskets to no more than 2/3 of capacity
    D. drain raw wet foods well before frying

6. Foods cooked incorrectly often lose flavor.
   When cooking beans or carrots, it is LEAST advisable to      6.____

    A. boil them in a small amount of water
    B. cook them in a steamer
    C. cook them in a pressure cooker
    D. cook them in an uncovered kettle

7. Of the following, the one which would make the LEAST satisfactory thickening agent in a casserole is      7.____

    A. wheat flour
    B. rice
    C. cornstarch
    D. tapioca

8. If baking powder biscuits do not rise to the proper height, the MOST probable cause is too      8.____

    A. *little* shortening
    B. *much* handling of dough
    C. *little* flour
    D. *much* baking powder

9. A soggy bottom crust in a lemon meringue pie is MOST probably caused by 9.____

   A. handling the crust too much
   B. baking at too high a temperature
   C. refrigeration of the crust prior to baking
   D. pouring in the filling when the pie is hot

10. The MOST appropriate type of poultry to purchase for chicken a la king is 10.____

    A. fowl       B. roasters       C. fryers       D. broilers

11. Of the following, Grade B eggs may be used MOST satisfactorily for 11.____

    A. poaching              B. scrambling
    C. frying                D. coddling

12. Considering both quality and economy, the BEST choice of the following grades to be specified when ordering apples for sauce is 12.____

    A. fancy                 B. extra fancy
    C. utility               D. U.S. #1

13. When submitting requisitions, the dietitian should give correct specifications for each item. 13.____
    Of the following items, the one which is CORRECTLY specified is

    A. celery - fresh, Grade A, trimmed, in boxes, 140 pounds
    B. oranges - fresh, commercial grade, size 75 to the half crate, 225 pounds
    C. salad greens - romaine, fresh, Grade A, trimmed, 30 pounds
    D. onions - dry, Grade A, in sacks, 200 pounds

14. The one of the following specifications which is INCOMPLETE is 14.____

    A. 200 lbs. of ham, 10 to 12 lbs. each, U.S. #1
    B. 120 lbs. fresh bottom rounds, 20 to 30 lbs. each, Choice
    C. 250 lbs. of boneless corned brisket, deckel removed, 10 to 12 lbs. each, Good
    D. 225 lbs. double veal legs, cut short, 40 to 48 lbs. each, Choice

15. Of the following food items, the one which does NOT have the correct varieties listed for it is 15.____

    A. melon - Honeydew, Cantaloupe, Persian, Casaba
    B. potatoes - Idaho, Cobbler, Russet, Yam
    C. onions - Spanish, Bermuda, Yellow, Red
    D. apples - McIntosh, Emperor, Delicious, Concord

16. Assume that you plan to serve 500 portions of beef stew, with 3 ounces of cooked meat in each portion. 16.____
    To provide this, you would need _____ lbs. _____ beef chuck.

    A. 95; boneless          B. 100; whole
    C. 125; boneless         D. 175; whole

17. You are serving buttered carrot rings on a menu for which you need 750 servings. 17.____
    The number of pounds of topped carrots you should order is MOST NEARLY _____
    lbs.

    A. 50   B. 75   C. 150   D. 300

18. Frozen broccoli is on the menu for dinner and you require 260 servings. 18.____
    The number of 2 1/2 lb. packages you would need is MOST NEARLY

    A. 10   B. 25   C. 50   D. 100

19. You wish to serve canned peas to 300 patients on the regular diet, 50 patients on bland 19.____
    diet, 35 patients on low fat diet, and 65 patients on light diet. Peas are supplied in #10
    cans, and these are ordered by the case only.
    The number of cases you would need is

    A. 1   B. 2   C. 3   D. 4

20. In order to ensure a minimum of leftover when you plan to serve 3 oz. portions of 20.____
    mashed potatoes to 500 persons, it would be BEST to order _____ potatoes.

    A. 40 lbs. instant
    B. 50 lbs. peeled
    C. 2 cases #10 cans of whole
    D. one 100 lb. sack of

21. The one of the following amounts which is MOST likely to yield 100 average servings is 21.____

    A. dry prunes, 25 lbs.
    B. bacon, sliced, rind removed (2 slices per serving), 20 lbs.
    C. coffee, ground for drip, percolator or silex, 2 lbs.
    D. egg noodles, buttered, 18 lbs.

22. The one of the following which would be INCORRECT to order when serving 200 per- 22.____
    sons is

    A. 8 #10 cans of applesauce
    B. 1 1/2 cases of #5 cans of tomato juice
    C. 100 lbs. of eviscerated fowl
    D. 20 lbs. of rice

23. To ensure that foods are relatively free of contamination when served in a cafeteria dur- 23.____
    ing a three hour meal period, it would be MOST advisable to

    A. stagger periods of preparation and service to the counter
    B. maintain a steam table temperature of 120° F
    C. reheat foods when they cool down
    D. eliminate all creamed foods from the menu

24. If egg salad has been prepared in a safe and sanitary manner, the criterion to be used to 24.____
    determine if it may be served one day later is that it

    A. still tastes good
    B. has a satisfactory general appearance
    C. still smells good
    D. has been continuously refrigerated

25. The one of the following statements concerning proper storage which is INCORRECT is  25.____
    that
    A. crates of eggs should be stored upright, never on ends or sides, because eggs are packed with the small end down
    B. crates of lettuce or fruit should not be stacked upright but on the side and should be cross-stacked to provide for air circulation
    C. fresh raw meat such as veal carcass should be carefully wrapped when stored to prevent contamination
    D. onions and potatoes do not require refrigeration; they are best stored in a dark, well-ventilated room at a temperature of 50° to 60° F

## KEY (CORRECT ANSWERS)

| | | | |
|---|---|---|---|
| 1. | D | 11. | B |
| 2. | B | 12. | C |
| 3. | C | 13. | C |
| 4. | C | 14. | A |
| 5. | A | 15. | D |
| 6. | D | 16. | C |
| 7. | C | 17. | C |
| 8. | B | 18. | B |
| 9. | D | 19. | C |
| 10. | A | 20. | D |

| | |
|---|---|
| 21. | C |
| 22. | D |
| 23. | A |
| 24. | D |
| 25. | C |

# TEST 3

DIRECTIONS: Each question or incomplete statement is followed by several suggested answers or completions. Select the one that BEST answers the question or completes the statement. *PRINT THE LETTER OF THE CORRECT ANSWER IN THE SPACE AT THE RIGHT.*

1. Of the following, the one which gives the LEAST desirable temperature for storing the item indicated is

    A. ripe bananas - 60° to 70° F
    B. fresh eggs - 53° to 58° F
    C. salad greens - 40° to 45° F
    D. fresh lamb - 33° to 38° F

    1.____

2. Of the following, the MOST important reason for requiring good ventilation in a storeroom is to prevent

    A. condensation of moisture
    B. roach or rodent infestation
    C. complaints from storekeepers about odors
    D. spoilage of canned goods

    2.____

3. Of the following foods, the one which is LEAST susceptible to insect infestation is

    A. dried beans
    B. dried fruits
    C. plain gelatin
    D. non-fat dry milk

    3.____

4. Of the following, the MOST effective measure for the elimination of rodents in a hospital kitchen is to

    A. clean the floors every day
    B. spread poison once a month in all allowable areas
    C. eliminate harborages
    D. screen off the slop sinks at all times

    4.____

5. Of the following ways to store food, it is LEAST desirable to place

    A. sacks of dried beans on racks
    B. cans of peas on the floor
    C. packages of cereal on shelves
    D. quarters of lamb on hooks in the refrigerator

    5.____

6. The MOST important reason for NOT overcrowding refrigerators is to

    A. make cleaning easier
    B. allow air circulation to reach all foods
    C. prevent waste resulting from overlooked foods
    D. reduce opportunities for pilferage of food

    6.____

7. Cooked foods should be cooled and refrigerated quickly, PRIMARILY to

    A. *prevent* growth and development of bacteria
    B. *preserve* food nutrients

    7.____

41

C. *prevent* loss of moisture content
D. *preserve* a *fresh cooked* appearance

8. In planning the layout of a kitchen, it is MOST important to arrange for

   A. grouping together of large pieces of equipment
   B. a separate work area for each cook
   C. a smooth and orderly flow of work
   D. separation of *wet* and *dry* areas

9. Of the following, the MOST satisfactory work surface for a cook's work table is

   A. hardwood 4" thick
   B. heavy gauge stainless steel
   C. heavy duty galvanized iron
   D. heavy gauge aluminum

10. Of the following, the practice which is LEAST advisable in the operation and maintenance of a food grinder is to

    A. hold the knife and plate in place by screwing the adjustment ring as tight as possible
    B. use a mallet to push pieces of food into the grinder
    C. remove the grinder plate and clean it thoroughly with a brush after each use
    D. remove the grinder head at the end of the day and clean all loose parts before storing them

11. The MAIN reason for selecting a cafeteria counter of standard fabricated units rather than a custom-built counter of the same quality is the

    A. lower initial cost
    B. easier cleaning
    C. greater flexibility for change and expansion
    D. lower maintenance costs

12. Of the following, the MOST suitable steam equipment for a main kitchen in a 100 bed hospital is

    A. one compartment steamer, one 80 gallon jacketed kettle, and one 60 gallon jacketed kettle
    B. two 30 gallon jacketed kettles and one 20 gallon jacketed kettle
    C. one 3 compartment steamer and two 30 gallon jacketed kettles
    D. two 2 compartment steamers and one 20 gallon jacketed kettle

13. The BEST choice for the top of a kitchen work table is

    A. 2 inch solid wood
    B. 12 gauge monel metal
    C. 20 gauge stainless steel
    D. galvanized metal

14. For equipment such as steam tables which require a water supply, it is MOST important to

    A. make sure there are no submerged inlets
    B. specify all stainless steel construction
    C. provide a heat booster
    D. supply both hot and cold water

14._____

15. In requisitioning a steam jacketed kettle, the LEAST important specification is that the

    A. draw off tube should be as close to the kettle as possible
    B. bottom should be pitched to facilitate run-off of contents
    C. kettle should be wall hung for easier cleaning
    D. draw off valve should be easily removable

15._____

16. The MAIN factor to consider when purchasing a slicing machine is the

    A. ease of cleaning
    B. adequacy of the safety guard for the cutting edge
    C. size of the machine in relation to the volume of slicing
    D. availability of replacement parts

16._____

17. In submitting your annual budget, you have requested a 2 drawer work table of complete stainless steel construction.
    If you are told that you must request a less expensive model, the MOST acceptable compromise for you to make would be to

    A. substitute ducoed legs with stainless steel feet
    B. substitute drawers of galvanized metal with stainless steel fronts
    C. specify a lighter weight stainless steel
    D. reduce the size of the table

17._____

18. The one of the following which is MOST likely to yield 100 average servings is

    A. fish filet - 30 pounds
    B. cream for coffee - 6 quarts
    C. oatmeal (rolled oats) - 5 pounds
    D. frozen spinach - 10 pounds

18._____

19. The one of the following requisitions which is NOT correct for 600 servings is

    A. 15 lbs. of ground coffee
    B. 9 lbs. of margarine chips for toast
    C. 3 #10 cans of jelly
    D. 60 lbs. of granulated sugar for cereal

19._____

20. You have requisitioned 8000 lbs. of beef carcass (650 to 700 lbs. per carcass). This will yield tender steaks, tender roasts, and less tender cuts for roasting, stewing, and chopping.
    Taking into account loss from trim, bones, and fat when the carcasses are processed, the amount of edible meat these carcasses should yield is MOST NEARLY _____ lbs.

    A. 4500   B. 5360   C. 6500   D. 7120

20._____

21. Analysis of the distribution of the average food dollar in a hospital can be of assistance to the dietitian in planning for and checking on the expenditure of funds.
Of the following, the MOST advisable distribution of funds for categories of food is:
meat, poultry, and fish _____%; dairy products _____%; fruits and vegetables _____%; bread and cereal _____%; miscellaneous _____%.

   A. 40; 20; 20; 10; 10
   B. 50; 10; 10; 10; 20
   C. 20; 20; 20; 20; 20
   D. 30; 30; 30; 5; 5

22. When planning a nutrition curriculum for the clinical instruction of student nurses, the factor which deserves the LEAST consideration is the

   A. educational purposes which the school of nursing seeks to attain
   B. educational experiences which are likely to meet the school's objectives
   C. service needs of the dietary department of the hospital
   D. methods of determining if the educational objectives have been attained

23. The current trend in the teaching of nutrition and diet therapy to student nurses emphasizes

   A. role playing and discussion groups as the most significant teaching devices
   B. instruction in food laboratories on preparation of foods
   C. instruction in food preparation and service to patients in the wards
   D. the clinical importance of diet therapy in a patient-centered plan of teaching

24. Suppose that the electric slicer used in the main kitchen is frequently out of order because of a short in the motor. The repair mechanic has demonstrated that this happens because excessive moisture is being used to flush out debris when cleaning the machine.
To prevent repetition of this breakdown, it would be MOST advisable to

   A. issue detailed written instructions on maintenance procedures to all cooks and kitchen employees who might have occasion to use or clean this slicer
   B. issue an order to all employees that no water is to
   C. be used when cleaning this slicer, only clean dry rags
   D. replace the slicer with a manual one that does not have a motor and, therefore, does not require electric current
   E. instruct two employees on each shift on the procedures to be used in cleaning the machine and restrict the use of the machine to them

25. Assume that a dietitian had instructed the kitchen helpers on how to minimize waste when preparing food for cooking. It would be MOST reasonable to conclude that such waste had been reduced subsequently if

   A. on a spot check, the employees observed were preparing the food as instructed
   B. operating costs for the dietary division during the next month were reduced
   C. the amount of food prepared during the next month decreased on a per capita basis
   D. requisitions of food supplies during the next month decreased

## KEY (CORRECT ANSWERS)

1. B
2. A
3. C
4. C
5. B

6. B
7. A
8. C
9. B
10. A

11. C
12. C
13. B
14. A
15. C

16. B
17. A
18. A
19. D
20. B

21. A
22. C
23. D
24. D
25. C

---

# EXAMINATION SECTION
# TEST 1

DIRECTIONS: Each question or incomplete statement is followed by several suggested answers or completions. Select the one that BEST answers the question or completes the statement. *PRINT THE LETTER OF THE CORRECT ANSWER IN THE SPACE AT THE RIGHT.*

1. A substance in food that nourishes the body is a(n)  1.____

    A. nutrient  B. calorie  C. enzyme
    D. antibiotic  E. capillary

2. Sugars and starches are included in which one of the following classes of nutrients?  2.____

    A. Fats  B. Proteins  C. Carbohydrates
    D. Minerals  E. Vitamins

3. The *most nearly* perfect food is  3.____

    A. eggs  B. milk  C. liver  D. fish  E. fruit

4. The process of heating milk to destroy harmful bacteria is  4.____

    A. pasteurization  B. homogenization  C. sterilization
    D. hydrogenation  E. fortification

5. Scurvy is caused by lack of vitamin  5.____

    A. A  B. B  C. C  D. D  E. E

6. Vitamin C is also called  6.____

    A. ascorbic acid  B. thiamine  C. niacin
    D. sunshine vitamin  E. riboflavin

7. The green coloring matter in plants is  7.____

    A. carotene  B. chlorophyll  C. carotenoid
    D. flavone  E. anthocyanin

8. _____ is NOT added to flour in the enrichment program.  8.____

    A. Thiamine  B. Riboflavin  C. Niacin
    D. Vitamin C  E. Iron

9. Pour batters include which one of these?  9.____

    A. Biscuits  B. Muffins  C. Waffles
    D. Dumplings  E. Coffee cakes

10. Gaseous substances which lighten or raise a batter or dough are called  10.____

    A. leavening agents  B. liquids  C. fats
    D. sugars  E. eggs

11. Which one of these are vine fruits?  11.____

    A. Strawberries  B. Grapes  C. Rhubarb
    D. Cherries  E. Pineapples

12. A flour which is a mixture of hard- and soft-wheat flours is _____ flour. 12._____

   A. bread   B. self-rising   C. all-purpose
   D. soft-wheat   E. hard-wheat

13. Quick breads are made tender by 13._____

   A. sugars   B. fats   C. liquids
   D. eggs   E. leavenings

14. The commercial test for freshness of eggs is called 14._____

   A. candling   B. washing   C. handling
   D. grading   E. sink or swim

15. A stimulant contained in cocoa and chocolate is 15._____

   A. theobromine   B. caffeine   C. theine
   D. tannic acid   E. kaffia

16. Raw or pasteurized milk which has the HIGHEST rating for purity and cleanliness and 16._____
    which is produced and marketed under strict supervision is

   A. grade A   B. pasteurized   C. certified
   D. homogenized   E. irradiated

17. Complete legumes are contained in 17._____

   A. green peas   B. corn   C. lentils
   D. soybeans   E. navy beans

18. Flour, liquid, salt, fat, sugar, and yeast are ingredients for 18._____

   A. quick breads   B. yeast bread dough   C. cakes
   D. pastry   E. cookies

19. Seasoned beef stock is 19._____

   A. bouillon   B. cream soup   C. bisque
   D. chowder   E. consomme

20. If a salad is served at the beginning of a meal, it is called a(n) 20._____

   A. appetizer   B. garnish   C. accompaniment
   D. main dish   E. substitute for a dessert

21. Milk, sugar, and eggs are the basic ingredients for 21._____

   A. starch puddings   B. steamed puddings   C. custards
   D. cakes   E. cookies

22. The leavening agent used in sponge and angel cakes is 22._____

   A. air   B. steam   C. baking powder
   D. soda   E. yeast

23. The CHIEF food value in fish is 23._____

   A. protein   B. fat   C. minerals
   D. vitamins   E. carbohydrates

24. A nutrient which is very low or absent in vegetables is                                                                24.____

    A. carbohydrates         B. minerals            C. vitamins
    D. fats                  E. cellulose

25. Frappes are                                                                                                           25.____

    A. cream or custard mixtures which are beaten during the freezing process
    B. sweetened fruit juices frozen to a mush
    C. fruit juices to which sugar and water have been added and the mixture frozen
    D. ices to which beaten egg whites have been added
    E. cream mixtures to which egg has been added

26. A protein contained in wheat which helps produce a light textured wheat bread is                                      26.____

    A. avidin                B. gluten              C. casein
    D. ovalbumin             E. ovoglobulin

27. The HIGHEST grade of beef which is tender, marbelized with fat, and readily cooked by                                 27.____
    broiling or roasting is

    A. utility               B. standard or commercial
    C. good                  D. choice
    E. prime

28. Trichinosis can be prevented by cooking                                                                               28.____

    A. pork until it is well done
    B. pork at a high temperature
    C. beef until it is tender
    D. beef at a high temperature
    E. fish at a low temperature

29. The ingredients necessary for making a standard pie crust are                                                         29.____

    A. flour, fat, liquid, and salt
    B. sugar, fat, flour, eggs, liquid, leavening agents, and flavoring
    C. flour, salt, baking powder, and liquid
    D. fat, sugar, flour, and flavoring
    E. fat, thickening agent, and a liquid

30. The following characteristics - level or slightly rounded on top, golden brown, velvety                               30.____
    crumb, even grain of fine texture, tender to touch and taste, and flavor well blended,
    moist, delicate, and sweet - describe a good

    A. muffin                B. biscuit             C. cake
    D. cookie                E. popover

31. To blanch means to                                                                                                    31.____

    A. moisten meats or other foods while cooking to prevent drying of the surface and to
       add flavor
    B. preheat in boiling water or steam and immerse immediately in cold water
    C. cook slowly with a small amount of water in a covered utensil
    D. coat with bread crumbs
    E. sprinkle or coat with flour or some other fine substance

32. To blend or to introduce air into a mixture by mixing thoroughly using an over-and-over motion is to

    A. beat    B. blend    C. cream    D. fold    E. stir

33. In one cup, there are _____ tablespoons.

    A. 4    B. 8    C. 16    D. 24    E. 32

34. The vitamin IMPORTANT in the prevention of beri-beri is

    A. thiamine    B. riboflavin    C. niacin
    D. ascorbic acid    E. vitamin A

35. Bartlett is a type of

    A. apple    B. peach    C. pear    D. apricot    E. plum

---

# KEY (CORRECT ANSWERS)

| | | | |
|---|---|---|---|
| 1. A | | 16. C | |
| 2. C | | 17. D | |
| 3. B | | 18. B | |
| 4. A | | 19. A | |
| 5. C | | 20. A | |
| 6. A | | 21. C | |
| 7. B | | 22. A | |
| 8. D | | 23. A | |
| 9. C | | 24. D | |
| 10. A | | 25. B | |
| 11. B | | 26. B | |
| 12. C | | 27. E | |
| 13. B | | 28. A | |
| 14. A | | 29. A | |
| 15. A | | 30. C | |

31. B
32. A
33. C
34. A
35. C

# TEST 2

DIRECTIONS: Each question or incomplete statement is followed by several suggested answers or completions. Select the one that BEST answers the question or completes the statement. *PRINT THE LETTER OF THE CORRECT ANSWER IN THE SPACE AT THE RIGHT.*

1. The part of the grain of wheat which contains MOST of the important nutrients is the    1.____

   A. bran  B. aleurone layer  C. endosperm
   D. germ  E. stalk

2. A _____ fact NOT characteristic of a good muffin baked at optimum temperature is    2.____

   A. good volume
   B. symmetrical shape with well-rounded top
   C. pebbled surface
   D. coarse grain
   E. thin crust

3. A moderate oven temperature is _____ degrees F.    3.____

   A. 250 to 300  B. 325  C. 350 to 375
   D. 400  E. 425 to 450

4. The type of wheat used in making macaroni products is    4.____

   A. durum  B. hard  C. soft
   D. all-purpose  E. whole

5. Blancmange is a    5.____

   A. soft custard
   B. baked custard
   C. type of ice cream
   D. pudding thickened with cornstarch
   E. gelatin dessert

6. _____ is a hard cheese.    6.____

   A. Limburger  B. Parmesan  C. Roquefort
   D. Cottage  E. Bleu

7. One of the ESSENTIAL nutrients contained in the leafy, green, and yellow vegetable group is    7.____

   A. vitamin A  B. vitamin D  C. riboflavin
   D. protein  E. iron

8. A nutrient NOT found in milk is    8.____

   A. calcium  B. protein  C. iron
   D. vitamin A  E. riboflavin

9. The CHIEF function of carbohydrates is to    9.____

   A. provide energy  B. promote growth
   C. protect health  D. build and regulate the body
   E. regulate body temperature

10. The sugar that occurs in milk is

    A. sucrose  B. lactose  C. glucose
    D. fructose  E. maltose

11. The building and regulation of the body is a function of

    A. sugars  B. fats  C. proteins
    D. minerals  E. starches

12. A mineral which is important for the development and functioning of hemoglobin in the blood is

    A. zinc  B. manganese  C. cobalt
    D. fluorine  E. iron

13. _____ is NOT a fat-soluble vitamin.

    A. A  B. C  C. D  D. E  E. K

14. A lack of vitamin A may cause

    A. night blindness  B. pellagra
    C. rickets  D. scurvy
    E. cirrhosis

15. A frozen dessert with a heavy whipped cream base and which is frozen WITHOUT beating or stirring is called

    A. ice cream  B. an ice  C. a sherbet
    D. a mousse  E. a frappé

16. Of the following foods, the one MOST suitable for a young child is

    A. pastry  B. pickles  C. sausage
    D. candies  E. custard

17. The space for each person, including silver, china, glassware, and napkin, is called the

    A. table  B. cover  C. place mat
    D. place setting  E. table setting

18. An example of American china is

    A. Royal Doulton  B. Spode  C. Minton
    D. Lennox  E. Wedgewood

19. A nondigestible carbohydrate found in the structural portions of all plants is

    A. cellulose  B. bran  C. ash
    D. glucose  E. starch

20. Calcium is important for

    A. the development of hemoglobin
    B. utilization of iron
    C. formation of sound teeth and bones
    D. formation of red blood cells
    E. hard dental enamel

21. An enlargement of the thyroid gland may be caused by a lack of

    A. iron    B. copper    C. cobalt    D. iodine    E. fluorine

22. The fifth group of the basic seven includes meat, poultry, fish, eggs, and

    A. leafy vegetables          B. citrus fruits
    C. milk                       D. grains
    E. dried peas and beans

23. Oil, vinegar, egg yolk or whole egg, and seasonings are ingredients found in

    A. French dressing           B. mayonnaise
    C. cooked salad dressing     D. fruit salad dressing
    E. Italian dressing

24. Chocolate is richer than cocoa in that it has MORE

    A. fat             B. protein        C. sugar
    D. carbohydrate    E. stimulants

25. A type of poisoning which gives no identifying sign and is caused by microorganisms present in improperly canned foods is called

    A. flat-sour       B. swell          C. botulism
    D. fermentation    E. putrefaction

26. A method of canning which can be successfully used for acid foods like fruits, tomatoes, and rhubarb is the

    A. hot water bath            B. pressure cooker
    C. vacuum pack               D. pickling method
    E. oven canning method

27. A jam that contains more than one kind of fruit and *usually* nuts or raisins is called

    A. fruit batter    B. conserves      C. jam
    D. marmalade       E. jelly

28. An important principle to remember in cooking vegetables is to

    A. cook in a small amount of water
    B. cook for a long time
    C. slice or cut in small pieces before cooking
    D. cook uncovered to retain food values
    E. add soda

29. Brains and sweetbreads are an example of

    A. leftover meats            B. muscle meats
    C. less tender cuts          D. variety meats
    E. tender meat cuts

30. When milk is irradiated, it has been fortified with

    A. vitamin D       B. protein        C. iron
    D. fat             E. vitamin C

31. To let food stand in French or other thin salad dressing until well-seasoned is to

    A. blanch
    B. blend
    C. cream
    D. marinate
    E. saute

32. Young chickens 8 to 12 weeks old and weighing 1 to 2 1/2 pounds are classed as

    A. broilers
    B. fryers
    C. pullets
    D. capons
    E. stags

33. The MOST delicate dinnerware is

    A. pottery
    B. earthenware
    C. china
    D. plastic
    E. paper

34. _____ are NOT considered as finger foods.

    A. Potato chips
    B. Olives
    C. Crackers
    D. Cookies
    E. Pies

35. The MOST important meal of the day is

    A. breakfast
    B. brunch
    C. lunch
    D. dinner
    E. supper

# KEY (CORRECT ANSWERS)

| | | | |
|---|---|---|---|
| 1. | D | 16. | E |
| 2. | D | 17. | B |
| 3. | C | 18. | D |
| 4. | A | 19. | A |
| 5. | D | 20. | C |
| 6. | B | 21. | D |
| 7. | A | 22. | E |
| 8. | C | 23. | B |
| 9. | A | 24. | A |
| 10. | B | 25. | C |
| 11. | D | 26. | A |
| 12. | E | 27. | B |
| 13. | B | 28. | A |
| 14. | A | 29. | D |
| 15. | D | 30. | A |

31. D
32. A
33. C
34. E
35. A

# TEST 3

DIRECTIONS: Each question or incomplete statement is followed by several suggested answers or completions. Select the one that BEST answers the question or completes the statement. *PRINT THE LETTER OF THE CORRECT ANSWER IN THE SPACE AT THE RIGHT.*

1. Which of these is NOT an example of shellfish?  1.____
   - A. Shrimp
   - B. Oysters
   - C. Clams
   - D. Lobster
   - E. Herring

2. A protein that contains all the essential amino acids is called  2.____
   - A. a complete protein
   - B. an incomplete protein
   - C. an inorganic salt
   - D. carotene
   - E. gluten

3. _____ can provide heat and energy for the body.  3.____
   - A. Carbohydrates and fats
   - B. Calcium
   - C. Vitamins
   - D. Water
   - E. Iron

4. The process by which food material taken into the body is converted into living tissue is called  4.____
   - A. digestion
   - B. nutrition
   - C. mastication
   - D. fermentation
   - E. defecation

5. To manipulate with a pressing motion accompanied by folding and stretching is to  5.____
   - A. baste
   - B. dredge
   - C. knead
   - D. render
   - E. scallop

6. Our MOST concentrated source of energy is obtained from  6.____
   - A. carbohydrates
   - B. fats
   - C. proteins
   - D. minerals
   - E. vitamins

7. A term used to measure the energy value of food is  7.____
   - A. calorie
   - B. B.T.U.
   - C. International Unit
   - D. gram
   - E. milligram

8. To harden the product, sterling silver contains a small percentage of  8.____
   - A. iron
   - B. zinc
   - C. copper
   - D. nickel
   - E. brass

9. Sage is an example of a(n)  9.____
   - A. spice
   - B. herb
   - C. flavoring
   - D. salt
   - E. oil

10. Linen tablecloths are made from fibers of  10.____
    - A. silk
    - B. cotton
    - C. flax
    - D. rayon
    - E. acetate

11. Cookies baked all together in a large pan and cut in squares or rectangles when cool are called  11._____

   A. drop
   B. bar
   C. press
   D. rolled
   E. refrigerator

12. The all-American favorite dessert is  12._____

   A. pie
   B. ice cream
   C. pie a la mode
   D. cake
   E. cookies

13. All of these are ingredients needed for cream pies EXCEPT  13._____

   A. egg
   B. milk
   C. thickening agent
   D. gelatin
   E. flavoring

14. Overmixing and overhandling are two mistakes to avoid in making  14._____

   A. pastry
   B. cookies
   C. yeast dough
   D. cakes
   E. frozen desserts

15. A fruit having the LEAST pectin is  15._____

   A. sour apples
   B. crab apples
   C. currants
   D. Concord grapes
   E. peaches

16. A method used MOST often for cooking steaks and chops is  16._____

   A. roasting
   B. broiling
   C. braising
   D. stewing
   E. pot-roasting

17. Eggs used in making mayonnaise are used  17._____

   A. for flavor
   B. for texture
   C. as a leavening agent
   D. as a coating
   E. as an emulsifying agent

18. When the shape of the fruit is to be preserved, the  18._____

   A. sugar is added at the beginning of the cooking period
   B. sugar is added just after the fruit has been softened
   C. sugar is added at the end of the cooking period
   D. fruit should be baked
   E. fruit should be broiled

19. The sugar MOST commonly used in cookery which is found in sugar cane, sugar beets, and the sap of maple trees is  19._____

   A. glucose
   B. dextrose
   C. fructose
   D. lactose
   E. sucrose

20. The flesh of calves less than 14 weeks old is called  20._____

   A. beef    B. veal    C. pig    D. lamb    E. mutton

21. Gelatin mixtures combined with whipped cream are called  21._____

   A. snows or sponges
   B. Spanish creams
   C. Bavarian creams
   D. Charlotte russe
   E. gels

22. Flatware includes all of the following EXCEPT 22.____

    A. bowls          B. knives           C. forks
    D. spoons         E. butter spreaders

23. The RICHEST source of vitamin E is 23.____

    A. wheat germ     B. meat             C. butter
    D. grains         E. egg yolk

24. A factor important in the control of clotting of blood is vitamin 24.____

    A. A      B. D      C. E      D. K      E. B

25. The MOST perishable meat of the following would be 25.____

    A. larger cuts of fresh, raw meat
    B. smaller cuts of fresh, raw meat
    C. frozen meat
    D. frozen meat which has been thawed
    E. cured meat

26. The base for all molded desserts is 26.____

    A. eggs           B. cornstarch       C. flour
    D. tapioca        E. gelatin

27. Overweight is *usually* NOT caused by 27.____

    A. too much of an unbalanced diet
    B. disturbance of the function of the glands
    C. an emotional problem
    D. eating between meals
    E. an appetite for rich foods

28. A main dish, dessert, and beverage is an example of a _____ luncheon. 28.____

    A. very light         B. light        C. moderate
    D. moderately heavy   E. heavy

29. When bone meal is added to fine china to give it strength, it is called 29.____

    A. pottery        B. semi-vitreous ware   C. china
    D. bone china     E. porcelain

30. Which description is NOT a characteristic of freezing? 30.____

    A. Quick and easy to do
    B. Leaves a product resembling fresh food in taste, color, nutritive value, and general appearance
    C. Destroys the enzymes, bacteria, molds, and yeast plants
    D. Delays spoilage until the food thaws
    E. Stops the growth of bacteria

31. A person recovering from an illness is called a(n) 31.____

    A. patient        B. convalescent     C. inmate
    D. invalid        E. inpatient

32. To cook in liquid just below the boiling point is to

   A. scald
   B. boil
   C. simmer
   D. steam
   E. pan-broil

33. Selecting each food separately in ordering a meal is known as menu

   A. a la carte
   B. table d'hote
   C. entree
   D. a la mode
   E. bonne femme

34. A condition caused by a lack of iron is

   A. cirrhosis
   B. night blindness
   C. anemia
   D. rickets
   E. beri-beri

35. Unfermented tea is called

   A. black
   B. green
   C. oolong
   D. orange pekoe
   E. gunpowder

## KEY (CORRECT ANSWERS)

| | | | |
|---|---|---|---|
| 1. | E | 16. | B |
| 2. | A | 17. | E |
| 3. | A | 18. | A |
| 4. | B | 19. | E |
| 5. | C | 20. | B |
| 6. | B | 21. | C |
| 7. | A | 22. | A |
| 8. | C | 23. | A |
| 9. | B | 24. | D |
| 10. | C | 25. | D |
| 11. | B | 26. | E |
| 12. | B | 27. | B |
| 13. | D | 28. | B |
| 14. | A | 29. | D |
| 15. | E | 30. | C |

| | |
|---|---|
| 31. | B |
| 32. | C |
| 33. | A |
| 34. | C |
| 35. | B |

# EXAMINATION SECTION
# TEST 1

DIRECTIONS: Each question or incomplete statement is followed by several suggested answers or completions. Select the one that BEST answers the question or completes the statement. *PRINT THE LETTER OF THE CORRECT ANSWER IN THE SPACE AT THE RIGHT.*

1. In the making of brown soup stock, a desirable and cheap cut of meat to use is     1.____

    A. shank of beef
    B. shoulder of veal
    C. brisket of beef
    D. end of round

2. To clarify a broth, it is advisable to     2.____

    A. add egg whites to hot stock and allow to cool
    B. add egg whites to cool stock and bring to boil
    C. strain stock frequently
    D. remove the scum which forms in cooking

3. Soda is used in the making of cream of tomato soup to     3.____

    A. improve the flavor
    B. thicken it
    C. neutralize the acid
    D. retain the color

4. Sauteing is cooking     4.____

    A. under the broiler
    B. by dry heat
    C. in deep fat
    D. in small amount of fat

5. Braising is cooking by     5.____

    A. dry heat
    B. moist heat
    C. broiling and then roasting
    D. sauteing and then simmering in liquid

6. A rack of lamb refers to     6.____

    A. the fore shoulder
    B. 6 ribs in one piece
    C. 8 ribs in one piece
    D. two sets of ribs

7. A "London Broil" is usually made from     7.____

    A. Porterhouse steak
    B. sirloin steak

C. chuck steak
D. flank steak

8. Picnic hams are obtained from the

    A. hind quarter
    B. loin
    C. fore quarter
    D. pressed scraps of leftover ham

9. The crown roast is usually taken from

    A. lamb
    B. veal
    C. pork
    D. beef

10. Hydrogenated fat is usually made from

    A. beef fat
    B. vegetable fat
    C. combination of pork and vegetable oil
    D. butter

11. Heavy cream contains_____ butter fat.

    A. 30%
    B. 40%
    C. 50%
    D. 60%

12. The white of egg beaten stiff, to which a small amount of sugar has been added, is called

    A. omelet
    B. fondant
    C. consomme
    D. meringue

13. The best apple to use for "baked apple" is

    A. Roma beauty
    B. Macintosh
    C. delicious
    D. greening

14. The term 20-30 applied to dried prunes denotes

    A. quality
    B. number to the pound
    C. space taken up in packing
    D. weight of box

15. "Marsh Seedless" is a term applied to

   A. oranges
   B. grapefruit
   C. raisins
   D. grapes

16. Vinegar is added to preserve the color in cooking of _____ vegetables.

   A. yellow
   B. green leafy
   C. white
   D. red

17. To make two gallons of coffee in an urn, the best amount of coffee to use is _____ lb(s).

   A. 1/2   B. 3/4   C. 1   D. 1-1/2

18. The best method for making tea is to

   A. pour freshly boiled water over tea
   B. place tea in cold water and bring to boil
   C. place tea into boiling water
   D. place tea into lukewarm water and then bring to boil

19. Baking powder biscuits should be baked in a

   A. cool oven
   B. hot oven
   C. cool, then increased to hot, oven
   D. moderate oven

20. Air is used as a leavening agent in

   A. sponge cake
   B. biscuits
   C. cookies
   D. bread

21. Yeast grows best in bread making in

   A. cold liquid
   B. boiling liquid
   C. lukewarm liquid
   D. cold liquid brought to boil

22. Puff paste is used in the making of

   A. éclairs
   B. sponge cake
   C. popovers
   D. Napoleons

23. Gelatin is obtained from

    A. apples
    B. cereals
    C. seawood
    D. tissue and bones of animals

24. A suitable utensil for both cooking and serving is

    A. double boiler
    B. platter
    C. casserole
    D. tureen

25. French service is

    A. service from platters to empty dish at table by waiters
    B. dishes made up individually in the kitchen and served by waiter
    C. entire meal made up on platters and placed on table in advance
    D. dishes made up at table by host and served by maid

---

# KEY (CORRECT ANSWERS)

1. A
2. B
3. C
4. D
5. B

6. A
7. D
8. C
9. A
10. B

11. B
12. D
13. C
14. C
15. D

16. B
17. C
18. A
19. B
20. A

21. C
22. D
23. D
24. C
25. A

# TEST 2

DIRECTIONS: Each question or incomplete statement is followed by several suggested answers or completions. Select the one that BEST answers the question or completes the statement. *PRINT THE LETTER OF THE CORRECT ANSWER IN THE SPACE AT THE RIGHT.*

1. Milk served for fluid consumption should be used not later than_____ hours from the date of pasteurization.   1.____

   A. 24
   B. 48
   C. 72
   D. 96

2. Pasteurization is the process of heating milk to a temperature of_____ degrees Fahrenheit for 30 minutes.   2.____

   A. 143
   B. 155
   C. 163
   D. 190

3. Spoilage of food in a can is manifested by   3.____

   A. discoloration of the label
   B. swelling of the can
   C. the high temperature of the can
   D. odor from the can

4. "Flat Sour" is a condition found in some canned goods in which there is   4.____

   A. acid decomposition without formation of gas
   B. gas formation
   C. corrosion
   D. leakage

5. Of the following, the most common impurity found in gelatin is   5.____

   A. zinc
   B. lead
   C. sulphur
   D. alcohol

6. According to the Sanitary Code, sausage or sausage meat shall be deemed adulterated if it contains   6.____

   A. insufficient water
   B. any cereal
   C. glucose
   D. lactose

7. The principal object of curing meat is to

   A. destroy all organisms that are present
   B. preserve it for future use
   C. improve the original quality
   D. add flavor

8. The most frequent danger against which to guard in cereals is

   A. mustiness
   B. mold
   C. insect infestation
   D. odor

9. The best way to differentiate between mouldy beef, which is unfit for food, and beef which has been aged, is that in aged beef one finds that the mould

   A. occurs only around the fat
   B. usually penetrates the tissues
   C. is almost entirely on the surface
   D. is lighter in color

10. The proper storage of canned goods requires that they be kept in a

    A. dry, cool place
    B. freezer
    C. dry, warm place
    D. damp place

11. Which does not contain caffeine or a caffeine-like alkaloid?

    A. Cocoa
    B. Coffee
    C. Chicory
    D. Tea

12. The sardine caught on the eastern seaboard is most closely related to the

    A. herring
    B. salmon
    C. mackerel
    D. cod

13. The food product which may not be sterilized by heating after processing, without significant damage to its marketable qualities, is

    A. ketchup
    B. orange juice
    C. mayonnaise
    D. mustard

14. Springers, a faulty product of the canning process, are due to

    A. leakage
    B. effective sterilization

C. inadequate sterilization
D. overfilling

15. The chemical most commonly used as a preservative in the United States is 15.____

    A. sodium benzoate
    B. salicylic acid
    C. sodium bicarbonate
    D. sodium chloride

16. One ton of frozen quarters will occupy approximately_____ cubic feet of space. 16.____

    A. 100
    B. 300
    C. 500
    D. 800

17. One ton of boneless frozen beef will occupy approximately_____ cubic feet of space. 17.____

    A. 25
    B. 50
    C. 100
    D. 150

18. The first neck bone is called the_____ bone. 18.____

    A. feather
    B. atlas
    C. pin
    D. ridge

19. The aitch bone is found in the 19.____

    A. round
    B. shoulder
    C. hip
    D. rib

20. The number of ribs in a beef side is 20.____

    A. 12
    B. 13
    C. 18
    D. 26

21. The pork knuckle and foot not separated is called a 21.____

    A. button
    B. hock
    C. lacone
    D. ribeye

22. United States government grading of meats shipped interstate is 22._____

   A. optional
   B. compulsory
   C. accepted
   D. ignored

23. Cod fat is found in the carcasses of 23._____

   A. bull
   B. stag
   C. steer
   D. cow

24. For raising hogs, all regions of the United States are considered to be 24._____

   A. suitable
   B. inadvisable
   C. partly suitable
   D. poor

25. The thin, paper-like covering over the outside of lamb or mutton is called 25._____

   A. skin
   B. cane fat
   C. fell
   D. dressing

## KEY (CORRECT ANSWERS)

1. C
2. A
3. B
4. A
5. B

6. B
7. B
8. C
9. B
10. A

11. C
12. B
13. B
14. C
15. A

16. B
17. D
18. B
19. C
20. B

21. B
22. A
23. A
24. C
25. D

# TEST 3

DIRECTIONS: Each question or incomplete statement is followed by several suggested answers or completions. Select the one that BEST answers the question or completes the statement. *PRINT THE LETTER OF THE CORRECT ANSWER IN THE SPACE AT THE RIGHT.*

1. Veal is derived from the young of the _____ species.  1.____

   A. ovine
   B. porcine
   C. bovine
   D. equine

2. Liverwurst is  2.____

   A. dry sausage
   B. domestic sausage
   C. sausage byproduct
   D. turkey byproduct

3. The number in the U.S. inspection stamp on meat denotes the  3.____

   A. date
   B. inspector
   C. establishment
   D. grade

4. Hard rolls are baked  4.____

   A. on the hearth
   B. without steam
   C. on pans
   D. in metal boxes

5. The unit employed to regulate the water temperature to be used in dough mixing is called  5.____

   A. tempering tank
   B. steam generator
   C. boiler
   D. ice jacket

6. In the United States the meat from young bovine animals not over _____ is known as veal.  6.____

   A. 6 months
   B. 12 weeks
   C. 80 pounds
   D. 150 pounds

7. Cake flour can be differentiated from bread flour inasmuch as it  7.____

   A. cakes in the hand when squeezed
   B. has a yellowish color

C. is drier
D. spreads more easily when used in dusting

8. In making high-ratio cakes calling for a high percentage of liquid and sugar, _____ should be used.

   A. compound
   B. lard
   C. emulsified shortening
   D. oleo-margarine

8.____

9. Puff pastry products should be

   A. baked immediately after makeup
   B. given a 30-minute rest period
   C. placed in proof-box at 90 degrees
   D. boiled

9.____

10. Enriched flour contains added

    A. minerals
    B. vitamins
    C. calories
    D. fat

10.____

11. Niacin, thiamine and riboflavin are

    A. vitamins
    B. calories
    C. enzymes
    D. carbohydrates

11.____

12. The mineral content of flour is determined by running a_____ test.

    A. gluten
    B. ash
    C. absorption
    D. protein

12.____

13. The temperature and relative humidity of a dough room should be _____°F.

    A. 60-65
    B. 65-70
    C. 75-80
    D. 80-90

13.____

14. A dough method in which all the ingredients are mixed in one operation is called_____ method.

    A. sponge
    B. Sauerteig
    C. straight
    D. soaker

14.____

15. The hearth of an oven is usually cleaned by   15.____

   A. washing with brush and water
   B. brushing
   C. swabbing
   D. soaking

16. How many one-pound loaves of baked pan bread will 112 1/2 pounds of dough make?   16.____

   A. 95
   B. 100
   C. 109
   D. 112 1/2

17. A machine which shapes the dough for pan bread is called   17.____

   A. divider
   B. rounder
   C. moulder
   D. proofer

18. To secure maximum expansion and gloss in bread,_____ is injected into the oven.   18.____

   A. steam
   B. cornmeal
   C. water
   D. carbon dioxide gas

19. The proper length of time for the baking of a one-pound loaf of bread is _____ minutes.   19.____

   A. 20-25
   B. 30-35
   C. 45-50
   D. 50-60

20. Sugar cookies of standard size, that is, 2 inches in diameter, require an oven heated to_____°F.   20.____

   A. 287
   B. 300
   C. 400
   D. 495

21. To thicken one quart of cherry fruit juice for pie filling,_____ ounces of pie thickener/cornstarch and tapioca is necessary.   21.____

   A. 2    B. 4    C. 6    D. 8

22. A pie dough which has been overmixed will result in a_____ crust.   22.____

   A. tender
   B. flaky
   C. tough
   D. soft

23. The clear sound product made from wheat flour by the removal of a large part of the starch is termed _____ flour.    23._____

    A. gluten
    B. clear
    C. patent
    D. whole wheat

24. In order to stabilize water, bakers have recourse to the use of    24._____

    A. ammonia carbonate
    B. baking soda
    C. mineral salts
    D. sodium chloride

25. The type of yeast mainly used by the baker of today is    25._____

    A. dry
    B. stock
    C. compressed
    D. barm

## KEY (CORRECT ANSWERS)

| | |
|---|---|
| 1. C | 11. A |
| 2. C | 12. C |
| 3. B | 13. D |
| 4. A | 14. A |
| 5. A | 15. A |
| 6. B | 16. D |
| 7. D | 17. C |
| 8. C | 18. C |
| 9. B | 19. D |
| 10. B | 20. B |

21. B
22. C
23. B
24. D
25. A

# TEST 4

DIRECTIONS: Each question or incomplete statement is followed by several suggested answers or completions. Select the one that BEST answers the question or completes the statement. *PRINT THE LETTER OF THE CORRECT ANSWER IN THE SPACE AT THE RIGHT.*

1. High-ratio layer cakes are baked at an oven temperature of_____°F.  1._____

    A. 290-300
    B. 325-335
    C. 380-390
    D. 425-450

2. A diet deficient in iron may be corrected by adding  2._____

    A. milk
    B. egg yolk
    C. enriched bread
    D. fruits

3. Lack of iodine in the diet may cause  3._____

    A. diabetes
    B. anemia
    C. goiter
    D. liver damage

4. Cellulose is important in food because it furnishes the body with  4._____

    A. energy
    B. roughage
    C. protein
    D. calcium

5. One serving (about one tablespoon) of butter yields_____ calories.  5._____

    A. 50
    B. 100
    C. 200
    D. 400

6. Butter is a good source of vitamin  6._____

    A. A          B. B          C. C          D. E

7. When macaroni with cheese is the main dish of a luncheon, to make a well-balanced meal one would choose  7._____

    A. bread and butter
    B. salmon salad
    C. fruit salad
    D. potato salad

2 (#4)

8. Scurvy is easily prevented by adding to the diet

   A. fats
   B. milk
   C. orange juice
   D. red meats

   8.____

9. Night blindness is probably due to a lack of vitamin

   A. A  B. B  C. C  D. D

   9.____

10. The flavor of Roquefort cheese is brought about by

    A. bacteria
    B. heavy cream
    C. chemicals
    D. molds

    10.____

11. Yeast is used in bread baking because it

    A. produces carbon dioxide
    B. forms a brown crust
    C. adds flavor
    D. adds softer texture

    11.____

12. Blanching is a term used in

    A. meat cutting
    B. canning
    C. baking
    D. stewing

    12.____

13. The softening of meats is brought about chiefly by

    A. warmth
    B. chemicals
    C. enzymes
    D. cooling

    13.____

14. When milk is pasteurized,_____ are killed.

    A. all bacteria
    B. some bacteria
    C. all harmful bacteria
    D. no bacteria

    14.____

15. The flavor of coffee is due chiefly to

    A. caffeine
    B. sugar
    C. origin of beans
    D. caffeol

    15.____

16. The highest grade of lard is_____ lard.

    A. kettle-rendered leaf
    B. prime steam
    C. refined
    D. heat treated

17. A filet is a piece of meat which is free from

    A. fat
    B. skin and bones
    C. connective tissue
    D. vital nutrients

18. A number 10 can of fruit serves approximately_____ persons.

    A. 8
    B. 15
    C. 23
    D. 35

19. Foods served by the waiter at the table from a container to the guest is called_____ service.

    A. A La Russe
    B. Butler
    C. French
    D. family style

20. Mace is another name for

    A. paprika
    B. cloves
    C. nutmeg
    D. thyme

21. An illustration of a condiment is

    A. cinnamon
    B. rice
    C. flour
    D. parsley

22. An entire meal for which the total price is fixed is called

    A. buffet
    B. table d'hote
    C. a la carte
    D. family style

23. The fertility vitamin is

    A. B  B. D  C. E  D. A

24. The most serious disease that may be gotten from improperly canned non-acid foods is  24._____

   A. typhoid
   B. tuberculosis
   C. botulism
   D. dysentery

25. The most practical way of eliminating rat infestation is  25._____

   A. elimination of rat harborages
   B. trapping rats
   C. using rat poisons
   D. fumigation

## KEY (CORRECT ANSWERS)

1. C
2. B
3. C
4. B
5. B

6. A
7. C
8. C
9. A
10. D

11. A
12. B
13. C
14. C
15. D

16. A
17. B
18. B
19. C
20. C

21. A
22. A
23. C
24. C
25. C

# HYGIENIC FOOD PREPARATION

Preparing safe, wholesome, nutritious, and appetizing food is an important job. As a person who is involved in the preparation of foods, you contribute greatly to the success of the establishment where you work, whether it's a sub shop, caterer, gourmet restaurant, fast-food operation, hospital, nursing home, or camp. The things you do (or don't do) can affect the safety of foods that are served to your customers, clients, or patients.
This booklet will bring to your attention the need for good personal hygiene and will show you why safe food preparation is in your hands.

### Bacteria

Bacteria are all around us and carry out a number of functions vital for life. Many are beneficial and are responsible for the fermented dairy and meat products we enjoy. Some bacteria cause food to spoil, but only a small percentage are harmful to us. Because bacteria are invisible to the naked eye, their existence and activities are often overlooked or ignored until problems occur.

Unlike plants and animals that are composed of many cells, bacteria are single cells. Each bacterium is self-sufficient and lives independently. Bacteria come in a variety of shapes and must be magnified 1,000 times to be seen. About 400 million bacteria clumped together would be approximately the size of a grain of sugar.

Bacteria grow in a unique way; they increase in numbers, not in size. Under ideal conditions, cell numbers can double every half hour; one becomes two, two become four, four become eight, and so on. Therefore, if you start with one bacterial cell, after 12 hours there would be as many as 33,000,000. The rate at which bacteria grow is different for each type of organism and is affected by many factors.

Bacteria get from place to place by hitchhiking and people are one of the principal carriers. Bacteria are transferred to foods from hands, dirty aprons, utensils, food contact surfaces, and equipment. They get into food where they can cause spoilage and sometimes illness. After investigating foodborne disease outbreaks, regulatory authorities found that poor personal hygiene of people working width food was responsible for 16 percent of the illnesses.

You may be asking yourself, "How can this happen?" Think about where you've been and what you've touched in the last few hours. You've cleaned up a spill, laced a shoe, talked on the telephone, emptied the garbage, brushed your hair, handled a dish, prepared food, and done many more things.

Did you wash your hands after you performed each of these jobs? If you didn't, you should have!

Some bacteria live in the folds and wrinkles of our skin, in our nose and throat, on our hair, and under our fingernaiis. Other bacteria are picked up from things we touch.

Some of these bacteria cause food poisoning when they get into foods, grow at warm temperatures (between $45°$ F and $140°$ F), and are eaten. Symptoms like headache, nausea, vomiting, cramps, and diarrhea occur after eating foods in which harmful bacteria have grown. These bacteria usually do not change the appearance, smell, or nature of the food, and only laboratory testing can determine whether they are present.

# Practice Good Personal Hygiene

You can take a few steps to prevent these harmful bacteria from getting into foods by practicing good personal hygiene.
- Bathe or shower *every day* before goingto work.
- Put on a clean uniform every day or as often as yours gets dirty.
- Wash your hands frequently-but always after:
  - using the bathroom,
  - eating or drinking,
  - smoking or chewing tobacco,
  - handling dirty plates or garbage,
  - working with raw foods,
  - touching other parts of your body like your nose, mouth, hair, and skin,
  - handling dirty utensils, objects or equipment, or before
  - returning to your work area.

The following pictures show how people help bacteria hitchhike from place to place, and how poor personal hygiene contributes to the contamination of food.

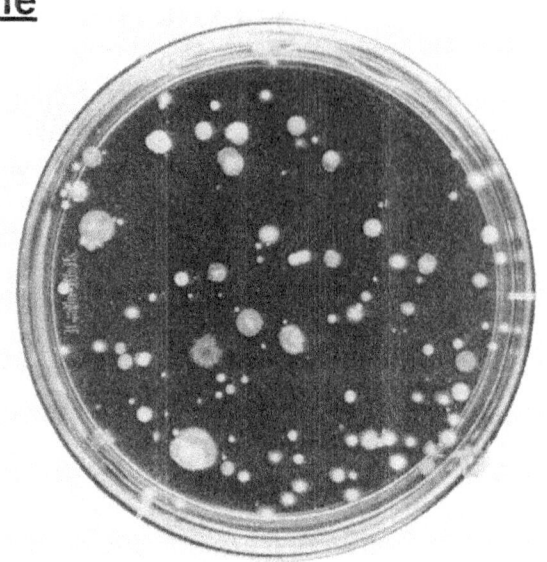

The bacteria grow rapidly by keeping them at a warm temperature (98.6° F). Twenty-four to 48 hours later, small colonies or clumps of bacteria approximately the size of a pinhead or larger can be seen in the agar.

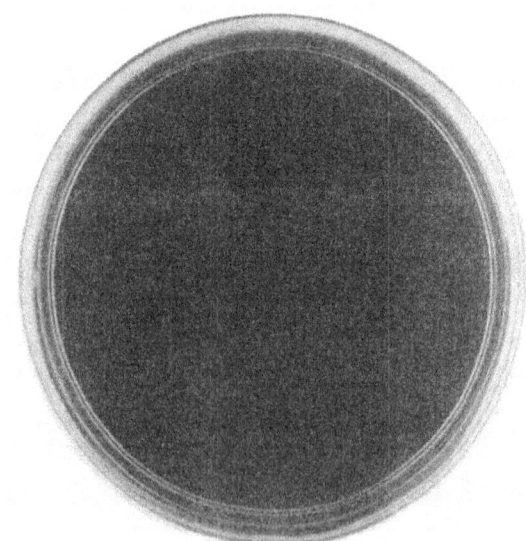

In the laboratory, bacteria grow on gelatin-like food (agar) in covered, sterile, plastic plates (petri dishes).

# Food Contaminants

**HANDS**

Let's see how hand washing affects the number of bacteria present.

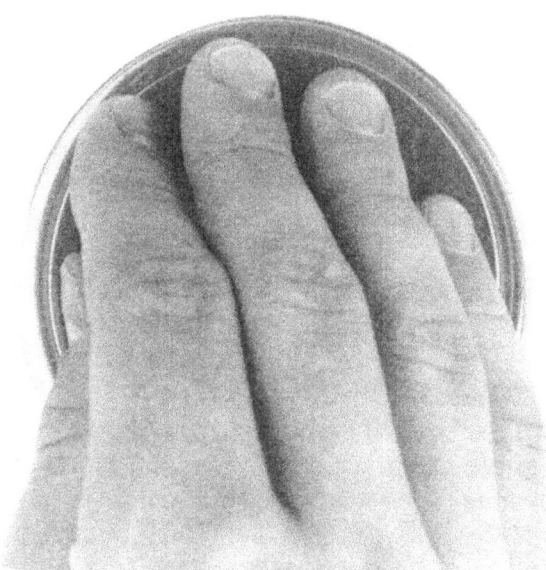

An unwashed hand that looks clean is touched to the agar.

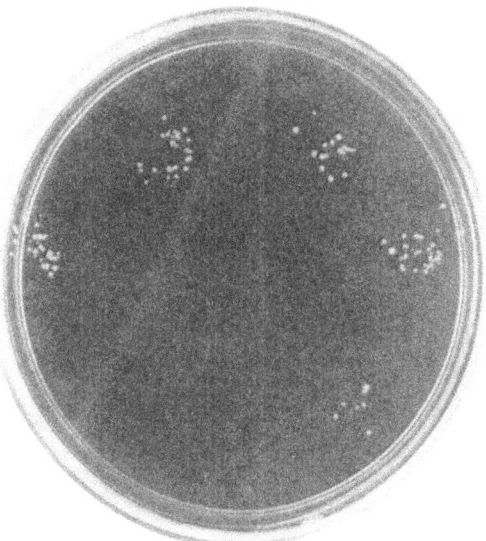

After washing hands for 15 seconds with hot water and soap, bacteria are reduced in number.

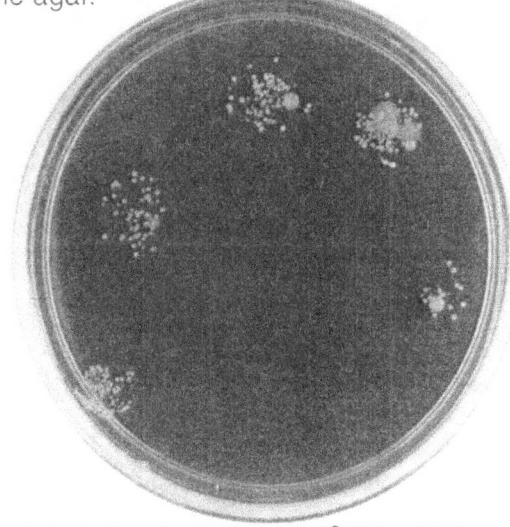

The plate is incubated at 98.6° F for 24 hours. The heavy growth of white colonies indicates that this hand was not very clean, and that millions of bacteria were present.

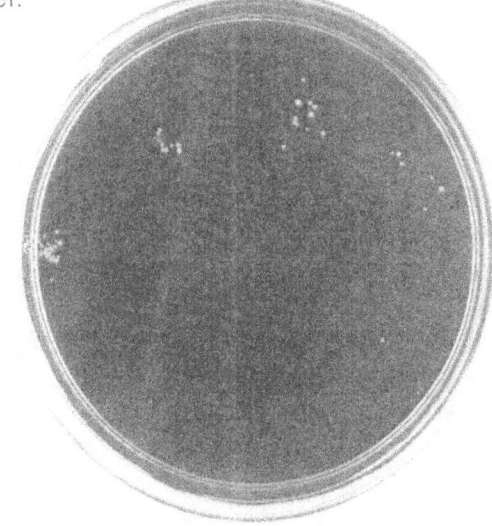

Washing the hands with soap and water for another 15 seconds reduces the bacteria even more.

After washing, the hands are not sterile because bacteria are hidden in the folds of the skin, but proper hand washing will significantly reduce the numbers of bacteria present.

Fingernails should be kept neatly trimmed and clean. Dirt harbors bacteria and gets under long or ragged nails.

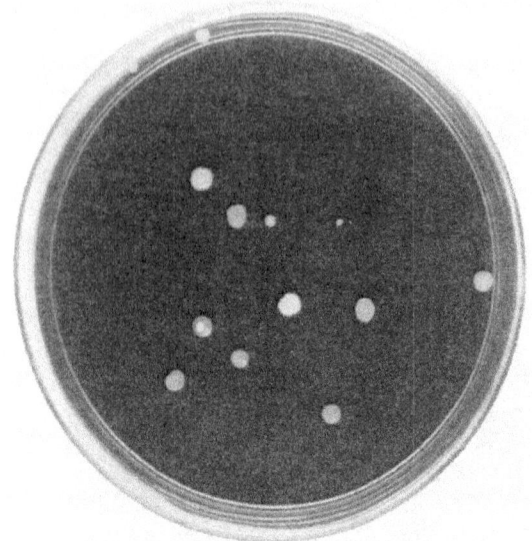

This picture shows the bacteria present in fingernail scrapings.

The main purpose of proper hand washing is to protect public health by preventing the transfer of disease-producing bacteria to foods. Although hand washing is a simple and easy task, you'd be surprised how many people avoid washing their hands or do it improperly. In several studies, it was estimated that nearly 60 percent of the people did not wash their hands after using the toilet. Disease-producing bacteria associated with human wastes can easily be transmitted to food if hands are not thoroughly and properly washed.

Sanitarians recommend the following hand-washing procedure for people working with food.

- Allow enough time to wash hands properly.
- Wet hands thoroughly in warm water (105° F).
- Apply a self-foaming soap, detergent, or disinfectant soap to the hands and lather all areas.
- Wash hands by rubbing one against the other using friction for 15-60 seconds. Particular attention should be given to the areas between the fingers and around the nails.
- Rinse off the cleaner and the soil under warm running water.
- Dry hands thoroughly with a clean, single service towel or a hot-air dryer.

In some food service establishments, after hand washing, hands are dipped into or sprayed with a sanitizing solution. Sanitizing hand creams can also be used. This further reduces the numbers of bacteria present. Sanitizers commonly used for the hands can be chlorine (50-100 ppm), iodophors (25 ppm), or quaternary ammonium compounds (QUATS) (200 ppm). These compounds should be checked frequently and changed when they lose their strength.

## LIPS AND NOSE

The lips and nose, in addition to hands, play an important role in harboring bacteria.

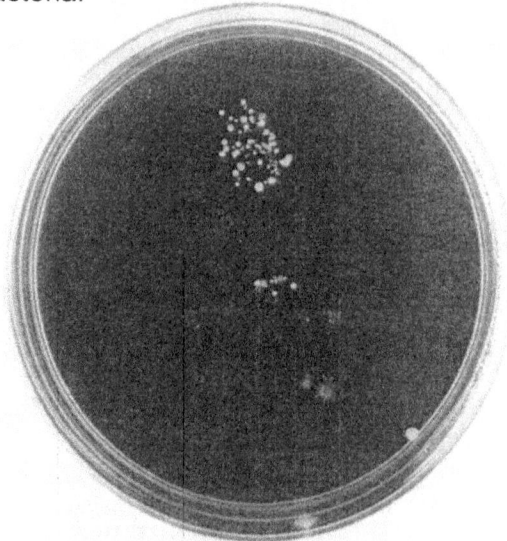

This plate shows what happens when the lips and nose are pressed against agar in a petri dish.

If someone smokes and then handles food, the tiny droplets of moisture from the mouth get transferred to the hands and find their way into the food. This is why smoking and chewing tobacco are not allowed in a food preparation area and why hands must be washed after smoking.

Bacteria also can find their way into food through coughs, sneezes, and vigorous nose blowing.

This picture shows that a single sneeze produces a mist of small droplets containing bacteria.

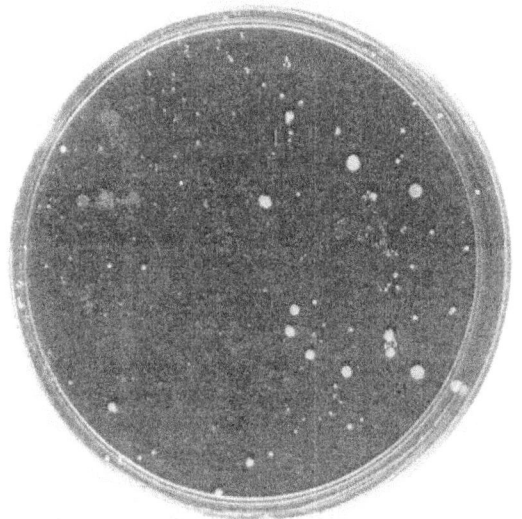

Each sneeze contains between 10,000 and 100,000 bacteria and they are moved through the air at more than 200 mph.

The mouth and nose should be covered when sneezing to prevent contamination of the foods being prepared. Always wash hands after coughing or sneezing.

### HAIR

Hair is also a source of bacteria and has no place in food. It is unappetizing, unappealing, and adds bacteria to food.

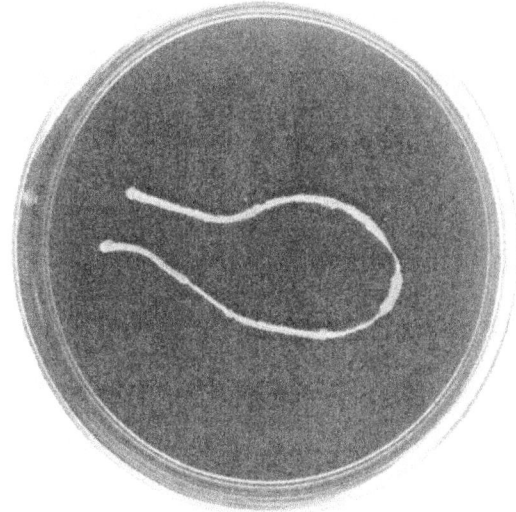

This picture shows the bacteria associated with human hair.

Since the average person loses 80 hairs a day, effective hair restraints must be worn to prevent hair from getting into food and to prevent food service personnel from brushing their hair and scratching their heads-which could result in harmful bacteria entering the food being prepared.

Washing the hair regularly and practicing good grooming techniques will help you look neat and clean, and will reduce the chances of bacteria entering food that is being prepared.

### DIRTY UTENSILS

Improperly cleaned and sanitized utensils also contribute to the contamination of food.

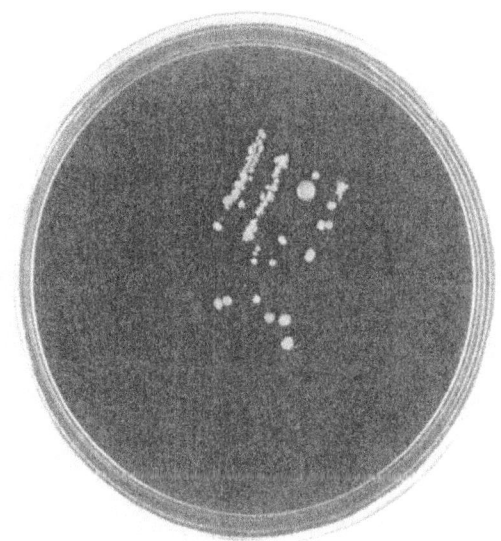

The above photo illustrates how an unclean fork adds millions of bacteria to food. Equipment and utensils must be washed thoroughly to remove soil, rinsed clean, and then sanitized.

Food safety and sanitation are a concern to everyone and it's up to each food industry worker to prevent foodborne disease. The safeness of food depends on all people, but especially those who produce and process it, transport and distribute it, and prepare it. Won't you do your part? Remember, Safe Food Preparation: It's In Your Hands!

# FOOD SERVICE GLOSSARY

## TABLE OF CONTENTS

| | Page |
|---|---|
| Absorption Capability ... Antioxidant | 1 |
| Antipasti or Antipasto ... Bavarian | 2 |
| Beat ... Brown | 3 |
| Brunswick Stew ... Chili con Carne | 4 |
| Chill ... Croutons | 5 |
| Crullers ... Disinfectant | 6 |
| Disposables ... Éclair | 7 |
| Edible ... Fold | 8 |
| Fold In ... Fricassee | 9 |
| Fritters ... Goulash | 10 |
| Gourmet ... Horseshoes | 11 |
| Host ... Kebab | 12 |
| Knead ... Marinade | 13 |
| Marinate ... Mulligatawny | 14 |
| Myocide ... Pare | 15 |
| Parkerhouse Rolls ... Potable | 16 |
| Potentially Hazardous pH ... Reconstitute | 17 |
| Rehydrate ... Saponify | 18 |
| Saturation ... Skim | 19 |
| Slack Dough ... Steep | 20 |
| Sterilize ... Tartar | 21 |
| Tarts ... Truss | 22 |
| Vacuum Drying ... Zwieback | 23 |

# FOOD SERVICE GLOSSARY

## A

**ABSORPTION CAPABILITY**
The property of flour to absorb and hold liquid.

**ACIDITY**
Sourness or tartness in a food product; in yeast doughs, a condition indicating excess fermentation; a factor in generating carbon dioxide for cake leavening.

**AERATION**
See LEAVENING.

**AEROBIC BACTERIA**
Those that require the presence of free oxygen as found in the air for growth.

**A LA CARTE**
On the menu alone, not in combination with a total meal.

**A LA KING**
A dish served with a cream sauce, usually containing green peppers and pimentos, and sometimes mushrooms and onions.

**A LA MODE**
In a fashion or the style of; for example, desserts served with ice cream or pot roast of beef cooked with vegetables.

**ALBUMEN**
Egg white.

**AMBROSIA**
A favorite southern dessert made of oranges, bananas, pineapple, and shredded coconut.

**AMEBA**
A simple animal-like organism that grows in water.

**ANAEROBIC BACTERIA**
Those that grow in oxygen-free atmosphere, deriving oxygen from solid or liquid materials and producing toxic substances.

**ANTIBIOTICS**
Substances produced by microorganisms and capable of inhibiting or killing other microorganisms.

**ANTIOXIDANT**
A chemical solution in which fruits and vegetables are dipped to prevent darkening.

### ANTIPASTI or ANTIPASTO
An appetizer, or a spicy first course, consisting of relishes, cold sliced meats rolled with or without stuffings, fish, or other hors d'oeuvres eaten with a fork.

### ANTISEPTIC
An agent that may or may not kill microorganisms, but does inhibit their growth. Peroxide is an example.

### APPETIZER
A small portion of food or drink before or as the first course of a meal. These include a wide assortment of items ranging from cocktails, canapes, and hors d'oeuvres to plain fruit juices. The function of an appetizer is to pep up the appetite.

### AU GRATIN
A thin surface crust formed by either bread or cheese, or both. Sometimes used with a cream sauce.

### AU JUS
With natural juice. Roast rib au jus, for example, is beef served with unthickened gravy.

## B

### BACILLI
Cylindrical or rod-shaped bacteria responsible for such diseases as botulism, typhoid fever, and tuberculosis.

### BACTERIA
Microscopic, one-cell microbes found in soil, water, and most material throughout nature. Some are responsible for disease and food spoilage, others are useful in industrial fermentation.

### BACTERICIDE
Any substance that kills bacteria and related forms of life.

### BAKE
To cook by dry heat in an oven. When applied to meats, it is called roasting.

### BARBECUE
To roast or broil in a highly seasoned sauce.

### BASTE
To moisten foods while cooking, especially while roasting meat. Melted fat, meat drippings, stock, water, or water and fat may be used.

### BATTER
A homogeneous mixture of ingredients with liquid to make a mass that is of a soft plastic character.

### BAVARIAN
A style of cooking that originated in the Bavarian section of Germany.

BEAT
   To make a mixture smooth or to introduce air by using a lifting motion with spoon or whip.

BENCH TOLERANCE
   The property of dough to ferment at a rate slow enough to prevent overfermentation while dough is being made up into units on the bench.

BLANCH
   To rinse with boiling water, drain, and rinse in cold water. Used for rice, macaroni, and other pastas to prevent sticking. For potatoes, to cook in hot, deep fat for a short time until clear but not brown.

BLAND
   Mild flavored, not stimulating to the taste.

BLEACHED FLOUR
   Flour that has been treated by a chemical to remove its natural color and make it white.

BLEEDING
   Dough that has been cut and left unsealed at the cut, thus permitting the escape of leavening gas. This term also applies to icing that bleeds.

BLEND
   To mix thoroughly two or more ingredients.

BOIL
   To cook in a liquid that bubbles actively during the time of cooking. The boiling temperature of water at sea level is 212° F.

BOTULISM
   Acute food poisoning caused by botulin (toxin) in food.

BOUILLON
   A clear soup made from beef or chicken stock or soup and gravy base.

BRAISE
   To brown meat or vegetables in a small amount of fat, then to cook slowly, covered, at simmering temperature in a small amount of liquid. The liquid may be juices rendered from meat, or added water, milk, or meat stock.

BREAD
   To coat with crumbs of bread or other food; or to dredge in seasoned flour, dip in a mixture of milk and slightly beaten eggs, and then dredge again in crumbs.

BROIL
   To cook under or over direct heat.

BROWN
   To cook, usually at medium or high heat, until the item of food darkens.

## BRUNSWICK STEW
A main dish composed of a combination of poultry, meats, and vegetables.

## BUTTERFLY
A method of cutting double chops (usually pork) from boneless loin strips. One side of each double chop is hinged together with a thin layer of meat.

## BUTTERHORNS
Basic sweet dough cut and shaped like horns.

# C

## CACCIATORE
Chicken cooked "hunter" style. Browned chicken is braised in a sauce made with tomatoes, other vegetables, stock, and herbs.

## CANAPE
Any of many varieties of appetizers, usually spread on bread, toast, or crackers and eaten with the fingers.

## CANDY
To cook in sugar or syrup.

## CARAMELIZED SUGAR
Dry sugar heated with constant stirring until melted and dark in color, used for flavoring and coloring.

## CARBOHYDRATES
Sugars and starches derived chiefly from fruits and vegetable sources and containing set amounts of carbon, hydrogen, and oxygen.

## CARBON DIOXIDE
A colorless, tasteless edible gas obtained during fermentation or from a combination of soda and acid.

## CARRIERS
Persons who harbor and disseminate germs without having symptoms of a disease. The individual has either had the disease at one time and temporarily continues to excrete the organism, or has never manifested symptoms because of good resistance to the disease.

## CHIFFONADE DRESSING
A salad dressing containing chopped hard-cooked eggs and beets.

## CHIFFON CAKE
A sponge cake containing liquid shortening.

## CHILI
A special pepper or its fruits. Dried, ground chili peppers are used in chili powder.

## CHILI CON CARNE
Ground beef and beans seasoned with chili powder.

**CHILL**
To place in a refrigerator or cool place until cold.

**CHOP**
To cut into pieces with a knife or chopper.

**CHOP SUEY**
A thick Chinese stew of thin slices of pork and various vegetables, such as bean sprouts, celery, and onions.

**CLEAR FLOUR**
Lower grade and higher ash content flour remaining after the patent flour has been separated. (Used in rye bread.)

**COAGULATE**
To thicken or form into a consistent mass.

**COAT**
To cover the entire surface of food with a selected mixture.

**CONDIMENTS**
Seasonings that in themselves furnish little nourishment, but which improve the flavor of food.

**CONGEALING POINT**
Temperature or time at which a liquid changes to a firm or plastic condition.

**COOKING LOSSES**
Loss of weight, liquid, or nutrients, and possibly a lowered palatability of a cooked food.

**COOL**
To let stand, usually at room temperature, until no longer warm to touch.

**CREAM**
To mix until smooth, sugar, shortening, and other ingredients; to incorporate air so that resultant mixture increases appreciably in volume and is thoroughly blended.

**CREAM PUFFS**
Baked puffs of cream-puff dough, which are hollow; usually filled with cream pudding, whipped topping, or ice cream.

**CREOLE**
A cooked sauce for poultry or shrimp. Usually served with rice.

**CRISP**
To make somewhat firm and brittle.

**CROUTONS**
Bread cut into small cubes and either fried or browned in the oven, according to the intended use. Used as a garnish, croutons are fried; as soup accompaniments, baked.

**CRULLERS**
   Long, twisted doughnuts.

**CRUMB**
   The soft part of bread or cake; a fragment of bread (see also BREAD).

**CRUST**
   Hardened exterior of bread; pastry portion of pie.

**CRUSTING**
   Formation of dry crust on the surface of doughs.

**CUBE**
   To cut into approximately 1/4 to 1/2 inch squares.

**CURDLE**
   To change into curd; to coagulate or thicken.

**CURING**
   A form of processing meat, which improves its flavor and texture.

**CURRY**
   A powder made from many spice ingredients and used as a seasoning for Indian and Oriental-type dishes, such as shrimp and chicken curry.

**CUSTOM FOODS (RATION-DENSE)**
   Various types of labor- and space-saving foods, including canned, concentrated, dehydrated, frozen, and prefabricated items.

**CUT IN (as for shortening)**
   To combine firm shortening and flour with pastry blender or knife.

## D

**DANISH PASTRY**
   A flaky yeast dough having butter or shortening rolled into it.

**DASH**
   A scant 1/8 teaspoon.

**DEVILED**
   A highly seasoned, chopped, ground, or whole mixture served hot or cold.

**DICE**
   To cut into 1/4 inch or smaller cubes.

**DISINFECTANT**
   A chemical agent that destroys bacteria and other harmful organisms.

## DISPOSABLES
Disposable articles used for food preparation, eating, or drinking utensils, constructed wholly or in part from paper or synthetic materials and intended for one single service.

## DISSOLVE
To mix a solid, dry substance with a liquid until the solid is in solution.

## DIVIDER
A machine used to cut dough into a desired size or weight.

## DOCKING
Punching a number of vertical impressions in a dough with a smooth round stick about the size of a pencil. Docking makes doughs expand uniformly without bursting during baking.

## DOT
To place small pieces (usually butter) on the surface of food.

## DOUGH
The thickened, uncooked mass of combined ingredients for bread, rolls, cookies, and pies, but usually applicable to bread.

## DOUGH CONDITIONER
A chemical product added to flour to alter its properties to hold gas.

## DOUGH TEMPERATURES
Temperature of dough at different stages of processing.

## DRAIN
To remove liquid.

## DREDGE
To sprinkle or coat with flour, sugar, or cornmeal.

## DRIPPINGS
Fat and juice dripped from roasted meat.

## DRY YEAST
A dehydrated form of yeast.

## DU JOUR
Today's or of the day; for example, Specialite du jour — food specialty of the day.

## DUSTING
Distributing a film of flour or starch on pans or work surfaces.

## E

## ECLAIR
A long, thin pastry made from cream puff batter, usually filled with cream pudding, whipped topping, or ice cream. The baked, filled shell is dusted with confectioner's sugar or covered with a thin layer of chocolate.

## EDIBLE
Fit to eat, wholesome.

## EMULSIFICATION
The process of blending together fat and water solutions of ingredients to produce a stable mixture that will not separate while standing.

## ENCHILADAS
A dish consisting of tortillas, a sauce, a filling (cheese, meat, or beans) and garnished with a topping such as cheese, then rolled, stacked, or folded and baked.

## ENRICHED BREAD
Bread made from enriched flour and containing federally prescribed amounts of thiamin, riboflavin, iron, and niacin.

## ENTREE
An intermediary course of a meal, which in the United States is usually the "main" dish.

## ENZYME
A substance, produced by living organisms, that has the power to bring about changes in organic materials.

## EXTRACT
Essence of fruits or spices used for flavoring.

# *F*

## FAT ABSORPTION
Fat that is absorbed in food products as they are fried in deep fat.

## FERMENTATION
The chemical changes of an organic compound caused by action of living organisms (yeast or bacteria), usually producing a leavening gas.

## FILET
The English term is "fillet," designating a French method of dressing fish, poultry, or meat to exclude bones and include whole muscle strips.

## FLIPPER
A can of food that bulges at one end, indicating food spoilage. If pressed, the bulge may "flip" to the opposite end. Can and contents should be discarded.

## FOAM
Mass of beaten egg and sugar, as in sponge cake before the flour is added.

## FOLD
To lap yeast dough over onto itself. With cake batter, to lift and lap the batter onto itself to lightly incorporate ingredients.

## FOLD IN
To combine ingredients gently with an up-and-over motion by lifting one up through the other.

## FOOD-CONTACT SURFACES
Those parts and areas of equipment and utensils with which food normally comes in contact. Also those surfaces with which food may come in contact and drain back into surfaces normally in contact with food.

## FOOD INFECTION
A food-borne illness from ingesting foods carrying bacteria that later multiply within the body and produce disease.

## FOOD INTOXICATION
Another term used synonymously with food poisoning, or the ingestion of a food containing a poisonous substance.

## FOOD POISONING
A food-borne illness contracted through ingesting food that contains some poisonous substance.

## FOOD VALUE
The quantity of a nutrient contained in a food substance.

## FOO YOUNG
A popular dish made with scrambled eggs or omelets with cut Chinese vegetables, onions, and meat. Usually, the dish is served with a sauce.

## FORMULA
A recipe giving ingredients, amounts to be used, and the method of preparing the finished product.

## FRANCONIA POTATOES
Potatoes are parboiled, then oven-browned in butter.

## FREEZE DRYING
Drying method where the product is first frozen and then placed within a vacuum chamber (freeze dehydration). Aided by small controlled inputs of thermal or microwave energy, the moisture in the product passes directly from the ice-crystalline state to moisture vapor that is evacuated.

## FRENCH BREAD
A crusty bread, baked in a narrow strip and containing little or no shortening.

## FRENCH FRY
To cook in deep fat.

## FRICASSEE
To cook by braising; usually applied to fowl or veal cut into pieces.

**FRITTERS**
Fruit, meat, poultry, or vegetables that are dipped in batter and fried.

**FRIZZLE**
To cook in a small amount of fat until food is crisp and curled at the edges.

**FRY**
To cook in hot fat. When a small amount of fat is used, the process is known as pan-frying or sauteing; when food is partially covered, shallow frying; and when food is completely covered, deep-fat frying.

**FUMIGANT**
A gaseous or colloidal substance used to destroy insects or pests.

**FUNGICIDE**
An agent that destroys fungi.

## G

**GARNISH**
To ornament or decorate food before serving.

**GELATINIZE**
To convert into a gelatinous or jelly-like form.

**GERM**
A pathogenic, or disease-producing bacteria. A small mass of living substance capable of developing into an organism or one of its parts.

**GERMICIDE**
A germ-destroying agent.

**GIBLETS**
The heart, gizzard, and liver of poultry cooked with water for use in preparing chicken or turkey stock or gravy.

**GLAZE**
A thick or thin sugar syrup or sugar mixture used to coat certain types of pastry and cakes.

**GLUTEN**
The elastic protein mass formed when the protein material of the wheat flour is mixed with water.

**GOULASH**
A Hungarian stew variously made in the United States of beef, veal, or frankfurters with onions and potatoes. The sauce has tomato paste and paprika as ingredients, served with sour cream if desired.

**GOURMET**
A connoisseur, or a critical judge, of good food and drink.

**GRATE**
To separate food into small pieces by rubbing it on a grater.

**GREASE**
To rub lightly with butter, shortening, or oil.

**GRIDDLE**
A flat surface or pan on which food is cooked by dry heat. Grease is removed as it accumulates. No liquid is added.

**GRILL**
See BROIL.

**GRIND**
To force food materials through a food chopper.

**GUMBO**
A Creole dish resembling soup, thickened somewhat with okra, its characteristic ingredient.

## H

**HARD SAUCE**
A dessert sauce made of butter and confectioner's sugar, thoroughly creamed. The mixture is thinned or tempered with boiling water.

**HASH**
A baked dish made of chopped or minced meat and/or vegetables mixture in brown stock.

**HEARTH**
The heated baking surface of the floor of an oven.

**HERMITS**
A rich short-flake cookie.

**HOLLANDAISE**
A sauce made with egg yolks and butter and usually served over vegetables.

**HONEY**
A sweet syrupy substance produced by bees from flower nectar.

**HORS D'OEUVRES**
Light, snack-type foods eaten hot or cold at the beginning of a meal.

**HORSESHOES**
Danish pastry, shaped like horseshoes.

**HOST**
  Any living animal or plant affording food for growth to a parasite.

**HOT CROSS BUNS**
  Sweet, spicy, fruity buns with cross-cut on top, which usually is covered with a plain frosting.

**HOT AIR DRYING**
  Products are cut in small pieces and spread on slat or wire bottom trays. Hot air is passed over and under trays to dry products.

**HUMIDITY**
  The percent of moisture in air related to the total moisture capacity of that air at a particular temperature. Usually expressed as relative humidity.

**HUNTER STYLE**
  Browned meat, usually chicken, braised in various combinations of tomatoes and other vegetables, stock, oil, garlic, and herbs.

**HUSH PUPPIES**
  Deep-fried cornbread batter seasoned with onions. Used mostly in the South, usually with fish.

## I

**INCUBATION PERIOD**
  That time between entrance of disease-producing bacteria in a person and the first appearance of symptoms.

**INSECTICIDE**
  Any chemical substance used for the destruction of insects.

**ITALIENNE**
  Italian style of cooking.

## J

**JARDINIERE**
  A meat dish or garnish, "garden" style, made of several kinds of vegetables.

**JULIENNE**
  A method of cutting meat, poultry, vegetables (especially potatoes), and fruits in long, thin strips.

## K

**KEBAB**
  Various Turkish-style dishes whose principal feature is skewered meat, usually lamb.

KNEAD
To work and press dough with the palms of the hands, turning and folding the dough at rapid intervals.

KOLACHES
A bread bun made from a soft dough and topped with fruit.

## L

LACTIC ACID
An organic acid sometimes known as the acid of milk because it is produced when milk sours. Bacteria cause the souring.

LARDING
To cover uncooked lean meat or fish with strips of fat, or to insert strips of fat with a skewer.

LASAGNA
An Italian baked dish with broad noodles, or lasagna noodles, which has been cooked, drained, and combined in alternate layers with Italian meat sauce and cheese of two or three types (cottage, parmesan, and mozzarella).

LEAVENING
The aeration of a product (raising or lightening by air, steam, or gas (carbon dioxide)) that occurs during mixing and baking. The agent for generating gas in a dough or batter is usually yeast or baking powder.

LUKEWARM
Moderately warm or tepid.

LYONNAISE
A seasoning with onions originating in Lyons, France. Sauteed potatoes, green beans, and other vegetables are seasoned this way.

## M

MAKEUP
Manual or mechanical manipulation of dough to provide a desired size and shape.

MARBLE CAKE
A cake of two or three colored batters partially mixed.

MARBLING
The intermingling of fat with lean in meat. Meat cut across the grain will show the presence or absence of marbling and may indicate its quality and palatability.

MARINADE
A preparation containing spices, herbs, condiments, vegetables, and a liquid (usually acid) in which a food is placed for a period of time to enhance its flavor, or to increase its tenderness.

**MARINATE**
 To cover with dressing and allow to stand for a short length of time.

**MARMALADE**
 A type of jam or preserve made with sliced fruits. Crushed fruits or whole fruits are used more commonly in jam.

**MEAT SUBSTITUTE**
 Any food used as an entree that does not contain beef, veal, pork, or lamb. Some substitutes are protein-rich dishes such as eggs, fish, dried beans, and cheese.

**MEDIA**
 The plural of medium.

**MEDIUM**
 A material or combination of materials used for cultivation of microorganisms.

**MELTING POINT**
 The temperature at which a solid becomes a liquid.

**MERINGUE**
 A white frothy mass of beaten egg whites and sugar.

**MILK FAT**
 The fat in milk and milk products.

**MILK LIQUID**
 Fresh fluid milk or evaporated or powdered milk reconstituted to the equivalent of fresh fluid milk.

**MINCE**
 To cut or chop into very small pieces, using knife or chopper.

**MINESTRONE**
 Thickened vegetable soup containing lentils or beans.

**MIXING**
 To unite two or more ingredients.

**MOCHA**
 A flavor combination of coffee and chocolate, but predominately that of coffee.

**MOLD**
 Microscopic, multicellular, thread-like fungi growing on moist surfaces of organic material.

**MOLDER**
 Machine that shapes dough pieces for various shapes.

**MULLIGATAWNY**
 A soup with a chicken-stock base highly seasoned, chiefly by curry powder.

**MYOCIDE**
An agent that destroys molds.

## N

**NUTRIENT**
A food substance that humans require to support life and health.

## O

**O'BRIEN**
A style of preparing sauteed vegetables with diced green peppers and pimientos.

**OLD DOUGHS**
Overfermented yeast dough that produces a finished baked loaf, dark in crumb color, sour in flavor, low in volume, coarse in grain, and tough in texture.

**OMELET**
Eggs beaten to a froth, cooked with stirring until set, and served in a half-round form by folding one half over the other.

**OVEN**
A chamber used for baking, heating, or drying.

**OYSTER MUSCLE**
Tender, oval piece of dark poultry meat found in the recess on either side of the back.

## P

**PALATABLE**
Agreeable to the palate or taste.

**PAN BROIL**
See BROIL.

**PAN FRY**
See FRY.

**PARASITES**
Organisms that live in or on a living host.

**PARBOIL**
To boil in water until partially cooked.

**PARE**
To trim and remove all superfluous matter from any article.

PARKERHOUSE ROLLS
Folded buns of fairly rich dough.

PARMESAN
A very hard, dry cheese with a sharp flavor.

PASTA (or PASTE)
Any macaroni product, including spaghetti, noodles, and the other pastas.

PATHOGENS
Disease-producing microorganisms.

PEEL
To remove skin, using a knife or peeling machine.

PEPPER POT
Any of a wide variety of styles of highly seasoned soup or stew.

PICKLE
A method of preserving food by a salt and water (or vinegar) solution.

PILAF
An oriental or Turkish dish made of rice cooked in beef or chicken stock and mildly flavored with onions.

PIQUANT
A tart, pleasantly sharp flavor. A piquant sauce or dressing contains lemon juice or vinegar.

PIT
To remove pits or seeds (as from dates or avocados).

PLASTICITY
The consistency or feel of shortening.

POACH
Method of cooking food in a hot liquid that is kept just below the boiling point.

POLONAISE
A garnish consisting of chopped egg and parsley served on cauliflower, asparagus, or other dishes. Bread crumbs are sometimes added.

PPM
Parts per million.

PORCUPINE
A preparation of ground beef and rice shaped into balls and cooked in tomato sauce.

POTABLE
Suitable for drinking.

## POTENTIALLY HAZARDOUS pH
Any perishable food which consists in whole or in part of milk or milk products, eggs, meat, poultry, fish, shellfish, synthetic food, or other ingredient capable of supporting rapid and progressive growth of pathogens.

## PREHEAT
To heat to the desired baking temperature before placing food in the oven.

## PROOF BOX
A tightly closed box or cabinet equipped with shelves to permit the introduction of heat and steam; used for fermenting dough.

## PROOFING PERIOD
The time between molding and baking during which dough rises.

## PROTOZOA
Minute, one-celled animals.

## PROVOLONE
A cured, hard cheese that has a smoky flavor.

## PSYCHROPHILIC BACTERIA
Microorganisms that grow at temperatures near freezing.

## PUREE
The pulp of a boiled food that has been rubbed through a sieve. Soup is called puree when it has been thickened with its sieved, pulpy ingredients.

## Q

## QUICK BREADS
Bread products baked from a lean, chemically leavened batter.

## R

## RABBIT OR RAREBIT
A melted-cheese dish.

## RAGOUT
The French word for "stew."

## RANCID
A disagreeable odor or flavor. Usually used to describe foods with high fat content, when oxidation occurs.

## READY-TO-COOK POULTRY
Drawn or eviscerated poultry.

## RECONSTITUTE
To restore the water taken from a food when it was dehydrated.

REHYDRATE
Combining a food with the same quantity of water that has been removed from it (see also RECONSTITUTE).

RELISH
A side dish, usually contrasting in color, shape, and texture to the meal. Usually designed to add flavor, zest, and interest to a meal.

RISSOLE
A French term meaning to obtain a crackling food by means of heat. Rissole potatoes are cooked to a golden brown crispness in fat.

ROAST
See BAKE.

ROPE
A spoiling bacterial growth in bread experienced when the dough becomes infected with bacterial spores. Poor sanitation can result in rope.

ROUNDING OR ROUNDING UP
Shaping of dough pieces into a ball to seal end and prevent bleeding and escape of gas.

ROUX
Preparation of flour and melted butter (or fat) used to thicken sauces, gravies, and soups.

ROYAL FROSTING
Decorative frosting of cooked sugar and egg whites.

## S

SAFE HOLDING TEMPERATURE
A range of cold and hot temperatures considered safe for holding potentially hazardous foods, including those refrigeration temperatures 40° F, or below, or heating temperatures 140° F, or above.

SALISBURY STEAK
A ground meat dish cooked with onions and made to resemble steak in shape. Sometimes referred to as hamburg steak.

SALMONELLA INFECTION
A type of food poisoning transmitted through foods such as poultry and poultry products containing salmonella bacteria.

SANITIZE
Effective bactericidal treatment of clean surfaces of equipment and utensils by an established process that is effective in destroying microorganisms.

SAPONIFY
To convert to soap.

**SATURATION**
Absorption to the limit of the capacity.

**SAUERBRATEN**
A beef pot roast cooked in a sour sauce variously prepared with spices and vinegar, and sometimes served with sour cream.

**SAUTE**
See FRY.

**SCALD**
To heat a liquid over hot water or direct heat to a temperature just below the boiling point.

**SCALE**
An instrument for weighing.

**SCALING**
Apportioning batter or dough according to unit of weight.

**SCALLOP**
To bake food, usually cut in pieces, with a sauce or other liquid.

**SCORE**
To cut shallow slits or gashes in the surface of food with a knife.

**SCORING**
Judging finished goods according to points of perfection; or to cut or slash the top surface of dough pieces.

**SEASON**
To add, or sprinkle, with seasonings or condiments.

**SHRED**
To cut or tear into thin strips or pieces using a knife or a shredder attachment.

**SIFTING**
Passing through fine sieve for effective blending and to remove foreign or oversize particles.

**SIMMER**
To cook in liquid at a temperature just below the boiling point.

**SKEWER**
A sharp metal or wood pin used to hold parts of poultry meat or skin together while being roasted.

**SKIM**
To remove floating matter from the surface of a liquid with a spoon, ladle, or skimmer.

**SLACK DOUGH**
 This is a dough that is soft and extensible but has lost its resiliency.

**SLIVER**
 To cut or split into long, thin pieces.

**SMOKING**
 A treatment used on most cured meat to add color and flavor.

**SMORGASBORD**
 A Scandinavian-type luncheon or supper, served buffet style. Many different dishes are served, including hot and cold hors d'oeuvres, pickled vegetables, fish, assorted cheeses, jellied salads, cold and hot fish, and meats.

**SMOTHER**
 To cook in a covered container, as smothered onions.

**SNAPS**
 Small cookies that run flat during baking and become crisp on cooking.

**SNICKERDOODLE**
 A coffeecake with a crumb topping.

**SOLIDIFYING POINT**
 Temperature at which a fluid changes to a solid.

**SPORE**
 Any one of various small or minute primitive reproductive bodies, capable of maintaining and reproducing itself. These are unicellular, produced by plants, molds, and bacteria.

**SPRAY DRYING**
 Used for liquids and thick materials such as soup. Hot air coming into a drier contacts the small globules of the product and causes the water to be evaporated.

**SPRINGER**
 A marked bulging of a food can at one or both ends. Improper exhausting of air from the can before sealing, or bacterial or chemical growth may cause swelling and spoilage.

**SPRINKLE**
 To scatter in drops or small particles, such as chopped parsley, over a finished product.

**STAPHYLOCOCCI**
 A family of bacteria formed in grapelike clusters, living as parasites on the outer skin and mucous membrane.

**STEAM**
 To cook in steam with or without pressure.

**STEEP**
 To let stand in hot liquid below boiling temperature to extract flavor, color, or other qualities from a specific food.

STERILIZE
To destroy microorganisms by chemical or mechanical means.

STEW
To simmer in liquid.

STIR
To blend or mix ingredients by using a spoon or other implement.

STREPTOCOCCI
Single-celled, globular-shaped bacteria.

STROGANOFF
Beef prepared with sour cream.

STRONG FLOUR
One that is suitable for the production of bread of good volume and quality.

SUCCOTASH
A combination of corn and lima beans.

SUGAR
To sprinkle or mix with sugar; refers to granulated unless otherwise specified in recipe.

SUKIYAKI
A popular Japanese dish consisting of thin slices of meat fried with onions and other vegetables, including bean sprouts, and soy sauce containing seasoning, herbs, and spices.

SWELLER
A can of food having both ends bulging as a result of spoilage. Swellers should be discarded, except molasses, in which this condition is normal in a warm climate.

## T

TABLEWARE
A general term referring to multi use eating and drinking utensils, including knives, forks, spoons, and dishes.

TACO
An open-face sandwich, Mexican style, made of fried tortillas shaped like a shell and filled with a hot meat-vegetable mixture.

TAMALE
A highly seasoned steamed dish made of cornmeal with ground beef or chicken rolled in the center.

TARTAR
A rich sauce made with salad dressing, onions, parsley, and sometimes pickle relish, olives, and cucumbers, served with fish and shellfish.

**TARTS**
Small pastries with heavy fruit or cream filling.

**TEMPERING**
Adjusting temperature of ingredients to a certain degree.

**TETRAZINNI**
An Italian dish with chicken, green peppers, and onions mixed in spaghetti and served with shredded cheese.

**TEXTURE**
The quality of the interior structure of a baked product. Usually sensed by the touch of the cut surface as well as by sight and taste.

**THERMOSTAT**
A device for maintaining constant temperature.

**THICKEN**
To transform a thin liquid into a thick one either by the gelatinization of flour starches or the coagulation of egg protein.

**TOAST**
To brown the surface of a food by the application of direct heat.

**TORTILLA**
A Mexican bread made with white corn flour and water. Special techniques are used in handling the dough to roll it thin as a pie crust. It is baked on an ungreased griddle or in the oven.

**TOSS**
To lightly mix one or more ingredients. Usually refers to salad ingredients.

**TOXIN**
A waste product, given off by an organism causing contamination of food and subsequent illness in human beings. It is the toxin of a disease-producing germ that causes the poisoning.

**TRICHINOSIS**
A food-borne disease transmitted through pork containing a parasite, Trichinella spirallis, or its larvae, which infects animals.

**TROUGHS**
Large containers, usually on wheels, used for holding large masses of raising dough.

**TRUSS**
To bind or fasten together the wings and legs of poultry with the aid of string or metal skewers.

## V

### VACUUM DRYING
Vacuum is applied to liquids and fills the liquid with bubbles, creating a puffing effect. The puffed product is then dried, leaving a solid fragile mass. This is then crushed to reduce bulk.

### VERMICELLI
A pasta, slightly yellow in color, shaped like spaghetti and very thin.

### VINAIGRETTE
A mixture of oil and vinegar seasoned with salt, pepper, and herbs, used in sauces and dressings.

### VIRUS
A group of organisms of ultramicroscopic size that grow in living tissue and may produce disease in animals and plants. Viruses are smaller than bacteria and, hence, pass through membranes or filters.

## W

### WASH
A liquid brushed on the surface of an unbaked or baked product (may be water, milk, starch solution, thin syrup, or egg).

### WATER ABSORPTION
Water required to produce a bread dough of desired consistency. Flours vary in ability to absorb water, depending on the age of the flour, moisture content, wheat from which it is milled, storage conditions, and milling process.

### WHEY
Liquid remaining after the removal of fat, casein, and other substances from milk.

### WHIP
To beat rapidly to increase volume by incorporating air.

## Y

### YEAST
A group of small, single-celled plants, oval in shape and several times larger than bacteria. Yeast helps to promote fermentation and is useful in producing bread, cheese, wine, and so on.

### YOUNG DOUGHS
Underfermented yeast dough producing finished yeast goods that are light in color, tight in grain, and low in volume (heavy).

## Z

### ZWIEBACK
A toast made of bread or plain coffeecake dried in slow oven.

www.ingramcontent.com/pod-product-compliance
Lightning Source LLC
Chambersburg PA
CBHW081829300426
44116CB00014B/2529